Just the Facts

Just the Facts

7 Steps of Conducting
Employment Investigations

Tommy T Bangani

WOODROCK
PUBLISHING

Project Manager: Fred van der Linde
Design and Layout: Ronel Niemand
Cover Design: Seamount Design
Editors: Roger Wanless & Westhouse Media

Printed in South Africa by Novus Print
First edition, First Printing, 2021

ISBN: 978-0-6398354-8-8

WoodRock Publishing
South Africa
www.woodrockpublishing.com

I dedicate this manual to the memory and contribution of all the workplace practitioners who made it possible for me to become the labour market professional that I am today.

And

To my children, who I seek to inspire by writing as a professional. I have not always had the time to be an active father in their lives due to professional commitments and other life challenges. I hope that they will forgive me for this omission, as I have always hoped that they become better than me – personally and professionally.

Contents

Acronyms ix
Reference Guide xi
Acknowledgements xv
Foreword xvii
To the Reader xxi
Brief description of book features xxix
Flowchart: Workplace Investigations xxxi

Section A: Laying the Foundation

Chapter 1 Access to Justice at work 3
Back to the Basics. The legal procedural framework
Chapter 2 Just the Facts 35
Processes, Systems and Procedures to investigate
Chapter 3 Legal Basis for an Investigation 51
Legal compliance. Conducting a flawless process

Section B: Building the Structure

Chapter 4 Organisational Preparation 73
Procedural Fairness. Getting the facts straight
Applying the AUDI Principle.

Chapter 5	An Investigator's Preparation Thoroughness. Terms of Reference compliance	91
Chapter 6	Handling an Investigation Meeting Objectivity. Managing Witnesses	125

Section C: Home of Best Practice

Chapter 7	Gathering Evidence Law of Evidence	147
Chapter 8	Involving Law Enforcement Services Organisational policy. Gross Misconduct	165
Chapter 9	Writing the Investigation Report Factual findings. Recommendations	175
Chapter 10	After Investigation is Completed Manage the aftermath. Improve culture	183
Chapter 11	Risk Mitigation Training Interventions Targeting financial and legal risks by identifying; analysing and managing employment issues before they escalate into disputes	189
Chapter 12	Key Concepts and Terms Application and Explanation of specific terminology	201

Appendices	225
Bibliography	245
Endnotes	247
About the Author	255

Acronyms

ABA –	American Bar Association (USA)
AGSA –	Auditor General South Africa
AWI –	Association of Workplace Investigators
BCEA –	Basic Conditions of Employment Act, nu 75 of 1997
CCMA –	Commission for Conciliation, Mediation and Arbitration
COIDA –	Compensation for Occupational Injuries and Diseases Act, nu 61 of 1997
CEO –	Chief Executive Officer
DOL –	Department of Labour (now Employment and Labour)
DG –	Director General
EEOC –	Equal Employment Opportunities Commission (USA)
EEA	Employment Equity Act, nu 55 of 1998
ETDP-SETA –	Education, Training and Development Professions Sector and Education Training Authority
FSCA –	Financial Sector Conduct Authority (Previously known as the FSB)
HAWKS –	Directorate for Crime Investigations, South Africa
HOD –	Head of Department
HRM –	Human Resource Management
HR / ER –	Human Resource / Employee Relations
ICT –	Information and Communication Technology

IES –	Inspections and Enforcement Services of the Department of Labour
LONMIN –	Lonmin plc, a producer of platinum metals operating in South Africa
LMIS –	Labour Market Information and Statistics Unit of the DoL
MEIBC –	Metal and Electrical Industries Bargaining Council, South Africa
LRA –	Labour Relations Act, 66 of 1995
NDPP –	National Directorate of Public Prosecutions, South Africa
NOSA –	South Africa's industry leader in occupational health, safety and environmental training
OHS –	Occupational Health and Safety
PSC –	Public Service Commission, South Africa
PSCBC –	Public Sector Coordinating Bargaining Council, South Africa
SACCAWU –	South African Commercial, Catering and Allied Workers Union
SAPS –	South African Police Service
SOP –	Standard Operating Procedure
SPA –	Single Point of Accountability
SAICA –	South African Institute of Chartered Accountants
SDA –	Skills Development Act
SMME –	Small Medium and Micro Enteprises
TOR –	Terms of Reference
UFS –	University of Free State

Reference Guide

Boxes

Box 1: Essential Characteristics of a Competent Investigator 50
Box 2: Framework for general workplace misconduct investigations 57
Box 3: Checklist for Managing the Investigation Process 69
Box 4: Securing Investigation Files and Records 114
Box 5: Determining the Credibility of a Witness 117

Letters

Letter inviting Ms Subramani the subject of the investigation 15
Letter informing affected person that an investigation has started 76
Investigation outcome letter 88
Model letter for inviting a suspect to interview meeting 115
Comprehensive outcome letter to complainant 155

Forms

Duty to cooperate advisement form 63
Investigation facts collection sheet 137
Grievance investigation notice 142
Notice to attend a grievance investigation meeting 152
Grievance investigation report 161

Practice Guides

Workplace investigation policy document 5
Workplace investigation framework 37
Workplace investigation methodology 42
Selection an investigation team 45
Checklist for managing the investigation process 69
Principles for conducting investigation interviews 81
Terms of reference document 93
Administrative suspension meeting script for management 100
Investigation report 108
Preliminary investigation plan 121
Guiding principles for conducting workplace investigations 128
Model workplace investigation case file 182
Security for investigation files and records 186
Fundamentals of conducting an employment investigation 188
Best practice employment investigation 199

Templates

Case investigation plan Investigation report	8
Model investigation plan	25
Investigation questionnaire	132
Workplace harassment investigation interview questions	149
Constituting an investigation file	163
Mistakes to avoid when conducting workplace investigations	173

Acknowledgements

I have had the privilege of conducting interviews – both on the record and informally - with many professionals and practitioners while doing research and writing this book. It is appropriate that I acknowledge those who contributed to my thinking by influencing my approach on the final product, which I take sole responsibility for.

Such persons include the following:

Aletta Van Tromp – Business Executive: Investigations at the Auditor General's Head Office in Pretoria who allowed me to have insight into the investigatory processes of the AGSA Office, into allegations and complaints of impropriety by public sector employees and managers.

Tsietsi Telite – Senior Manager: Coaching, Office of the AGSA, Pretoria who has been a sounding board for my ideas.

Zola Tshatshelo – Director: Supply Chain Management, Office of the Public Service Commission, South Africa who shared critical information on the investigation of misconduct by the PSC

Zwelihle Vice Ngonyama – MEIBC Manager, Gauteng who kindly engaged me as a workplace practitioner, in order to share good practice on conducting workplace investigations from a private sector bargaining council perspective.

To all the workplace practitioners who coached, guided and showed me the ropes when I was a novice and fresh from academic studies in the early 1990s, lacking practical experience. They include the following:

Amos Mothapo, SACCAWU National President, who gave me an opportunity to become a professional trade unionist, thus kindling my scholarly interests in workplace issues.

Mzwandile Mafenuka, SACCAWU Western Cape Leader, who showed me how to relate to a national employer as a negotiator, thus giving me insight into how an employer operates his business.

Twelve Fudumele, SACCAWU Western Cape Official, who taught me the tricks to survive in a highly politicised organisation, thus teaching me how to navigate corporate intrigues as a professional.

Zoë Holland, SACCWU Para Legal Officer, who introduced me to the theory and practice of labour law when there was no school of trade unionism to learn best practice strategies and tactics at the time.

Willard Nodlela, SACCAWU Western Cape Official, who taught me the basic skills to negotiate terms and conditions of employment as a union official.

I will always be grateful to all of them, including other workplace leaders and officials who are too numerous to mention by name. As fellow citizens who have since passed on, may all their souls rest in peace until we meet again.

Foreword

I first met Tommy Bangani while we were both working for the SA Commercial, Catering and Allied Workers Union in the early 1990s. He was based in Cape Town at the Western Cape Provincial Office as Regional Secretary, whilst I was working at the National Head Office in Gauteng as the Deputy General Secretary.

Tommy's theoretical base, workplace experience as a trade union official and an employee relations specialist qualify him as a thought leader on the subject matter of this book.

Both the Commission for Conciliation Mediation and Arbitration (CCMA) and the sector bargaining councils of South Africa are overloaded with dismissal and unfair labour practice cases. Most of these cases could have been prevented had there been proper investigation at the point of origin of the incidents. As Chief Executive Officer of Breakeven59 Pty Ltd I also serve as part-time senior commissioner of the CCMA. And it is my professional opinion that both a lack of requisite expertise and an appetite for investigative work has resulted in our dispute settlement institutions being paralysed by an unnecessary high caseload. I am alive to the central issues this book raises and the thorough research and investigation showcased in it.

An adversarial 'rights-based' mindset, where the reliance is on adjudicative processes (without competent investigation), as opposed to consensus seeking solutions, dominates decision-making around incidents of misconduct. Often quick-fix solutions are employed to address sensitive and intricate matters that cover human rights and social justice. There is no care, discernment or tact involved in the investigating of each individual case.

Therefore this book is a timely intervention to steer practitioners and managers of conflict resolution toward better practices and social justice. The *7 Steps of Conducting Employment Investigations* is an invaluable tool for practitioners. The same can be said for the other resources included in the book, in the form of case studies, letters and forms, practice guides, and templates.

The call for the institutionalisation of a professional body is worth serious consideration. Employers and employee representatives need continuous training and retraining to ensure that knowledge and the necessary skills to do investigative work are consistently updated. Competency in investigative work will greatly enhance the management of conflict and minimize the risk of labour law disputes.

Just the Facts is a solid contribution to labour law practice and a notable step towards a move away from quick-fix and adversarial approaches to employment relations. The book calls for a mind-set shift in conducting employment investigations. Bringing back credibility and professionalism to the employment investigation process is essential if practitioners and decision-makers are serious about obviating reputational and financial damage to organisations.

This book is a "must read" and a valuable tool for all practitioners in the private and public sectors.

Kaizer Thibedi

Part-time senior commissioner of dispute prevention and management at the Commission for Conciliation, Mediation and Arbitration (CCMA).
Johannesburg
10th December 2019

To the Reader

Conducting legally compliant workplace investigations is a professional activity. Internationally, it entails activities such as managing financial and reputational employment risks; complying with labour and human rights laws; investigating complaints and allegations against employees as well as grievances raised by employees. In this way the practitioners are ensuring access to justice for all at workplaces. In practice, this process is the primary responsibility of HR and ER practitioners, attorneys, forensic and auditing investigators as well as multidisciplinary specialists who seek to build a better workplace.

Still, even though South Africa has been a constitutional democracy since 1994 and the country has been using the Labour Relations Act, 66 of 1995, as amended (the Act) as an instrument to manage the employment relationship, conducting workplace investigations has not been fully built into the theory and practice of employment relations management. As a result, there is a dearth of information, knowledge and skills on how to use international best practice to conduct employment investigations. Furthermore, it is this best practice gap that makes it difficult for a national workplace investigation 'community of practice' to develop, in order to contribute to the emergence of a civilised and decent workplace.

Nevertheless, the Fair Procedure provision in item 4(1) of the *Code of Good Practice: Dismissal* in Schedule 8 of the Act is the starting point for any employer who seeks to conduct a legally compliant workplace investigation. It is the many cases of organisational failure to comply with this advice that has prompted the author to write this book. The overall purpose is to close the gap between theory and practice, on the interpretation and application of the provisions of Item 4 (1) of the *Code of Good Practice: Dismissal* in Schedule 8 of the LRA, 66 of 1995 which says that 'normally the employer should conduct an investigation'.

Again, many workplace practitioners – if not the majority – who draft disciplinary Charge Sheets that can lead to the dismissal of employees for alleged misconduct or poor work performance, have limited professional capabilities regarding the conduct of workplace investigations. To illustrate:

1. In the course of conducting research in preparation for this book - between 2014 and 2017 - I discovered that there is no accredited and professionally structured course on conducting employment investigations in South Africa*

2. I also learnt that most of the related training courses were about handling disciplinary hearings or OHS matters, with a small part dealing with conducting workplace investigations. In some books written by labour law experts, the subject of workplace investigations was dealt with in one page

3. Additionally, the contents of such training courses were inadequate when compared to what is the norm in the international jurisdictions researched

In practice, workplace practitioners were not familiar with key issues such as doing a preliminary assessment of allegations before conducting the actual investigation; understanding the legal and policy context of the organisation; deciding who should be the investigator based on their skills as a professional; ensuring that there are written terms of reference as well as complying with timeframes as provided for in a collective bargaining agreement. This list of critical workplace investigation considerations is not exhaustive.

South African case law illustrates how all of the above issues become the subject of litigation. In order to confirm the veracity of this analysis, one has merely to read annual reports from the bargaining councils, the CCMA and the Labour Court or even the Public Service Commission, in order to see the actual workplace dispute trends.

It is against the background that I conceptualised, designed and wrote this book. Put differently, the seven steps investigation platform that is the intellectual fountainhead of this book is intended to address all the above issues.

Each chapter is written in a fashion intended to impart skills to the practitioner. Thus, there is no recommended approach to reading the book. The reader can start with the last Section (C), if she is interested in writing an Investigation Report, or go straight to Section (B) if she wishes to design an Investigation Plan. Alternatively, you can also commence at the beginning, in Section (A) if you are interested in the basics of conducting a legally complaint workplace investigation. All the issues raised in the book are what usually emerge as points of contention when the respective parties present their cases at the various labour dispute resolution forums described above.

More importantly, my approach to writing the book is linked to the hopes, fears and dreams of practitioners. I know what it feels like to lose a case due to failure to get the basics right from the beginning. I have worked as an employment relations practitioner for more than (15) fifteen years. The last four of those fifteen years were spent within a government department where I was employed as a Director: Employee Relations. It was in this environment where I was convinced that practitioners need workplace investigation skills since none of the practitioners I worked with then had ever been trained as professional workplace investigators.

Rather, their approach to procedural fairness was mostly a result of 'trial and error' and hoping that the other party did not discover the flaws in the employer processes.

As a result, the outcome of an investigation was never communicated to the affected person as required by international best practice - if there ever was an investigation - to begin with! This anomaly is typical of many workplaces across the private sector and the public service in our country. This is confirmed by the lack of scholarly articles written by professionals and research documents from academia that talk directly to conducting best practice workplace investigations in South Africa.

In addition, there are very few Investigation Protocols that can be referenced by a practitioner when the need to conduct a workplace investigation arises. This is despite the existence of the Act and its attendant Code of Good Practice which advises that if there is a possibility of an employee being dismissed from employment, the employer is required to investigate. This is good practice, not compulsion by the lawmakers.

Nevertheless, it is this gap between theory and practice in South Africa that drove me to research what is being done in jurisdictions such as Australia, Canada, Europe, the UK and the USA. All these jurisdictions have professionalised the conduct of workplace investigations. Indicative of this sophisticated approach, there exist communities of practice in the form of an Association of Workplace Investigators or an equivalent professional body with a legal mandate. Thus, the professionalization of conducting workplace investigations is supported by practitioners, academia and employers in all the above countries. Surely, there are good lessons for South Africa to learn therefrom.

Lastly, I have taken a conscious decision to use case studies to illustrate the points I am making, in order to support my arguments for conducting legally compliant workplace investigations. The reader will notice that there are five 'true to life' case studies in the book. The said case studies address the following matters:

- *General Misconduct*, including insubordination; refusal to carry out a legitimate instruction; abuse of sick leave or use of employer property without permission
- *Financial Misconduct*, including misappropriation of assets; embezzlement; fraud; dishonesty and other economic crimes
- *Workplace Harassment*, including bullying; sexual harassment and victimisation
- *Terms and Conditions of employment grievances*, including employer refusal to promote on merit; failure to pay out a bonus and other workplace issues
- *Executive abuse of authority complaints*, relating to alleged nepotism and/or promotion of incompetent and underqualified 'inner circle' employees

The analytical arguments are then supplemented by tools and instruments that I have included in order to show workplace practitioners how to integrate into their daily professional life the various skills associated with conducting a workplace investigation.

This manual is an introduction to a distinct professional skill required for successfully managing the employment relationship. The book aims to clarify and explain a complex subject in a step-by-step manner that integrates theory and practice. A multitude of best practice tools and instruments are included in the text in the form of case studies, as well as explanations of key concepts and terms that are used frequently by workplace investigators.

The primary objective of sharing both the theory and practice is to ensure that the employer minimises the risk of labour law disputes. These disputes are usually caused by failure to comply with the applicable laws, prescripts, policy and collective bargaining agreements used as governance documents in the South African workplace.

This book is also about the interpretation of the meaning and practical application of Item 4 (1) of the *Code of Good Practice: Dismissal* in Schedule 8 of the Labour Relations Act, 66 of 1995 (the current Act). When an employer organisation takes a decision to dismiss an employee through an internal process (a disciplinary hearing), it must make sure that it can legally defend such a decision by showing 'just cause'. When the decision to dismiss is made, the employer should be prepared to handle the process in such a way as if it is expected that the decision will later be challenged by an employee representative or a legal practitioner at one of the Bargaining Councils, or the CCMA.

As a manual, this book will show practitioners how to conceptualise, design, conduct and manage a workplace investigation, from the beginning until its conclusion, when the investigator submits a written report to the leadership of the organisation for them to make a final decision.

Throughout the book the author seeks to share methodological approaches a practitioner can utilise during each of the seven steps involved in conducting a legally compliant workplace investigation.

Lastly, the final chapter of the book promotes the training of practitioners as an empowerment initiative in order to mainstream workplace investigations. Here the preferred model to be used for internal capacity building is informed by Doug Malouf's[1] TELL / SHOW / DO

/ REVIEW model of learning and teaching adults and/or professionals. It is this approach to capacity building for professionals that will ensure that the investigation report contains all the key ingredients, including; an executive summary, the terms of reference, allegations to be investigated, findings of fact as well as the recommendations regarding a way forward for the employer in addressing the matters under investigation.

Tommy Thamsanqa Bangani

Centurion, City of Tshwane

30 August 2019

Brief description of book features

Appendices and boxes:

Provide guidance to the practitioner on the methodology, strategy and tactics for conducting workplace investigations.

Chapter extracts: an opening statement that draws the attention of the reader to highlights to be focused on in the individual chapter.

Letters:

Constitute the proof that there has been communication between the employer organisation, the parties to the investigation and the investigator. They are to be included in the investigation case file.

Forms:

Facilitate the administration of the investigation process as they are part of the records to be kept by the employer, separate from the final report. They are additional proof that the investigator complied with the letter and spirit of the legal provisions on procedural fairness and further show transparency on the part of the employer.

Key concepts and terminology:

These are listed alphabetically, to ensure that practitioners build a common vocabulary as members of a professional 'community of practice' known as workplace investigators.

Practice guides:

Are best practice tools and instruments designed to drive the investigation process, from the commencement until its completion.

Process flow charts:

Is the essence of the theory and practice for conducting best practice employment investigations. This is the quality assurance for legal compliance and procedural fairness in conducting workplace investigations.

Structure and table of contents:

Is the navigator that guides the reader on how to approach the reading of the book. The theme and summary column list the key points per chapter.

Templates:

Show the practitioner how to apply the theory; they also assist in preparing a case file as they can be used as 'exhibits' in the event of a legal dispute at an independent labour dispute resolution forum.

As a workplace practitioner, miss reading this book at your own disadvantage.

Process flowchart

Workplace Investigations

PHASE 1:
Preliminary Analysis of Issue(s)

PHASE 2:
Develop an Investigation Plan

PHASE 3:
Collect Information and Evidence

PHASE 4:
Interview Witnesses

PHASE 5:
Analysis and Review of Evidence

PHASE 6:
Make Fact Findings and Draw Conclusions

PHASE 7:
Write Investigation Report and Manage Aftermath

Section A

Laying the Foundation

Chapter 1

Access to Justice at Work

Back to the Basics. The legal procedural framework

"Access to justice is the ability to obtain legal information, advice and assistance; access to courts, tribunals and alternative dispute resolution mechanisms; to obtain knowledge, advocacy and support, and participate effectively in law reform processes."

- Law and Justice Foundation of New South Wales (LJFNSW), 2014.

Introduction

In a constitutional democracy such as the Republic of South Africa, where the rights of citizens are enshrined in a *Bill of Rights*, it is accepted legal practice to work on the basis of the principle which says that 'everyone is presumed innocent, until proven guilty' by either a court of law or a civil legal dispute resolution forum. This is particularly the case in respect of employment or workplace matters, which is what this book focuses on.

This chapter sets the tone for the rest of the book by clarifying the application of the principle referred to above as it applies to the primary parties to the workplace relationship, namely the employer and the employee. HRM and/or employment relations practitioners and their associates are generally faced with legal challenges relating to the following issues:

1. Allegations of misconduct at work
2. Allegations of poor work performance
3. Accusations about the violation of national employment laws.

These relate to issues of health and safety or employment equity law provisions, including public and social policy guidelines developed to deal with allegations of sexual harassment at work, discrimination, bullying and retaliation, victimisation as well as scapegoating.

Historically, all the above allegations and accusations generally lead to disputes between the employer and its employees. As a result, the parties then go through a process of internal hearings, conciliation, mediation and arbitration or adjudication by a court of law in order to resolve the disputes. Statistically, these workplace disputes are shown to be increasing annually, as reported by the CCMA, Bargaining Councils and the Public Service Commission[1].

Escalating labour disputes are thus a concern. Many of the employment law matters that end up as disputes could have been resolved before reaching that stage, if practitioners knew the basics of conducting a legally compliant employment investigation. These situations affect access to justice at work for many employees. Most employees do not know how to deal with the absence of an investigation before a dismissal and find this a challenge. This is not surprising, given the complexities involved in addressing workplace matters later at disciplinary hearings.

Practice Guide

Workplace Investigation Policy Document

Contents

Part 1: Introduction
General Overview

Part 2: Guiding Principles
Independence
Impartiality
Fairness
Confidentiality

Part 3: Investigating
Purpose
Role of Investigator
Duty to Cooperate
Access to Records, Documents and Workplace
Anonymous Allegations
Timing of Investigation
Preliminary Inquiry
Formal Investigation
Interim Administrative Actions
Notification to Subject
Notification to Supervisors
Notification to Representatives
Gathering Documents and Other Pertinent Information

Part 4: Interviews
Deciding who to Interview
Location of Interviews
Conduct of Interviews
Records of Interviews

Part 5: Findings and Conclusions
Findings and Conclusions
Malicious, Frivolous and Vexatious Allegations

Part 6: Reporting
Investigation Report
Release of Investigation Report
Reporting to Organisational Officials
Reporting to External Auditors
Reporting to National Authorities
Security of Information

Part 7: After the Investigation
Communication Plan
Decision Making
Implementation of Recommendations
Training Interventions

In this chapter, we will learn to minimise the risk of labour law disputes by ensuring that practitioners comply with international best practice, our country's employment laws, employer policy guidelines and collective bargaining agreements. Accordingly, this will improve the employer's reputation among employees and other stakeholders observing the conduct of the key parties to the employment relationship. The following ten pillars[2] are built into the foundation in order to ensure that there is access to justice for both employer and employee.

Pillar 1. Ensure Procedural Fairness

Passing the procedural fairness test in cases of workplace misconduct dismissals is a key determinant of whether a dismissed employee can be reinstated or reemployed; whether an unfairly dismissed employee can be paid compensation or not; and whether an employer's reputation might be impaired for flouting the rules of natural justice. In this regard, there is more than enough case law emanating from the Labour Court, CCMA or Bargaining Councils to show the risk to the employer if they fail to comply with the requirements of procedural fairness.

The starting point though is for the employer to ensure that it defines the purpose of the investigation in terms that are legal as well as designed to 'test allegations or suspicions, to find out what really happened, and to establish whether there are grounds for disciplinary action'[3].

Secondly, it is also required that the investigator be appointed promptly by the employer, in line with the legal principle which says that 'justice delayed is justice denied'. Many practitioners are aware of reported cases where an employer has failed to comply with its negotiated Disciplinary Code and Procedure because it has appointed an investigator months after the fact, when it is required to do so within days of becoming aware of the alleged act(s) of misconduct.

Template

Confidential

Case Investigation Plan

Case No: ____________________

Date: ____________________

Business Unit/Directorate/Function: ____________________

SPA for Investigation: ____________________

Investigation Leaders (if not SPA): ____________________

- Name of Investigation Leader/person in charge of the investigation including their contact details

Investigation Team (if any):

____

____

____

Decision maker and (if any) Appeal Authority:

____

- Names and contact details of those who will act as decision makers after the investigation is concluded including those who will implement any disciplinary process triggered by the investigation findings
- Names and contact details of those who (if any) will hear any appeal lodged against the decisions taken

- Decision makers and those who may hear an appeal should not be directly involved in the progress of the investigation. In that way their objectivity – in taking any subsequent decision or hearing any appeal – can be preserved and they cannot be perceived as being "tainted" in their decision making. This means they should not be given any information of substance about the investigation until the investigators present their final report

Investigation Subject(s):

____

____

- Name and contact details of those whose conduct is being investigated

Complainant (unless stated as anonymous or highly confidential):

____

____

- Name of person(s) who raised the complaint
- How the complaint was raised
- Can the complainant be interviewed?
- Are there any special considerations to be considered when interviewing the complainant

Allegations:

- List all the allegations / facts reported by the complainant
- Name of Code of Conduct and Ethics section, company policy or employment standard and/or labour law violated
- Location of a copy of the relevant code, policy or employment standard

- Any employer standards or practices that are relevant to the allegations, how they can be best understood to work in practice and/or how any documents, standards or practices can be gathered
- What information / documents / evidence needs to be gathered relating to the allegations/facts?
- Location of relevant information / document

Background / Context:

- Any background facts/events/prior investigations relevant to this investigation?

Reasons for the Investigation and Issues Raised

e.g., theft, regulatory, inappropriate behaviour, fraud, bribery

The Communication Plan:

- Identifies those persons who have a "need to know" privilege
- Distinguishes between those who require a full update, as against those who only require an update on progress and/or outcome
- Sets out the manner, detail and frequency of communication to those parties
- Identifies those who should receive limited or no information (e.g., because they might have an actual or perceived conflict of interest)
- Addresses what information will be given to the complainant and when, including what the complainant will be told of the outcome of the investigation

Immediate Steps:

Any immediate administrative actions, e.g., suspension of individuals, transfer or regular notifications which need to be given

Chronological narration:

If helpful set out a chronology of events as known at the outset. Include dates, times, place, meetings, calls, conversations. Update this as the investigation proceeds

Investigation Approach:

- List of individuals to be interviewed
- Order in which they will be interviewed
- List of who will interview each interviewee and who will take notes. If only one person is to be conducting the interview and taking notes, then this should be stated
- Documents/evidence to be shown / discussed with each interviewee
- Which specific issues are to be covered with each interviewee

In many instances the employee representative will allow non-compliance to continue, with the tactical approach being to challenge it as an *injustice* at a later dispute meeting, either at a Bargaining Council or at the CCMA. It is more critical that, as part of the procedural fairness requirement, the employer inform an employee that there is an investigation underway that is looking into allegations of misconduct against them. This is in order to ensure that employees do not claim to have been ambushed if and when a decision to bring allegations of misconduct against them is proffered. Again, this is not a legal requirement, but it is advisable in order to avoid unnecessary disputes. This will minimise litigation that could otherwise be exceedingly costly financially and damaging to the reputation of the employer.

Pillar 2. Select Investigators Carefully

Analytically and procedurally, the investigation of alleged violations of public and social policy relating to health and safety issues at work is dissimilar to an inquiry into failure to comply with legal prescripts regarding employment equity in a specific workplace context. The former may be undertaken by a government agency such as the Department of Labour or a Bargaining Council with jurisdiction and called an inspection, whilst the latter can be done by an internal or external workplace investigator. In any event, it is important that the employer appoint an investigator who is above reproach and who has the following critical skills and professional competencies:

- Knowledge of the industry/sector

  It is common cause that employment challenges vary across a sector / industry. In addition, workplace investigation matters are different in the private sector as compared to the public service which is highly regulated. For instance, there are stringent policies to be complied with before an employee is dismissed for misconduct in the public service - due to high levels of unionisation. On the other hand, many employees are regularly dismissed in other sectors as there are no collective bargaining agreements regulating terms and conditions of employment, as a result of low levels of unionisation. So, an effective investigator must know all of this in order to be able to discharge his duty as a professional.

- Knowledge of the workplace

  A competent investigator appointed to investigate an event or incident at a gold mine must be able to differentiate his approach when appointed to investigate issues in the financial services sector (bank, insurance company, or an investment house). The first workplace, the mine, is labour intensive and known for having more than one union, whereas the other is technology driven and largely employs professionals. It is therefore not advisable to adopt a 'one size fits all' approach when conducting workplace investigations in any one of the many workplaces and/or in different organisations.

- An understanding of the legal process

Knowing the correct procedure the South African Police Service will follow when there is a criminal investigation of alleged corruption is not the same as knowing what is required to be done in the retail-distributive sector when an employee is suspected of financial misconduct relating to breaking into a warehouse and removing company property without authorisation.

In the one instance it could be a case of immediate suspension for fear of interference with internal processes, while the other case could be dealt with differently. Again, it is important to be aware of these nuances. They determine an approach to the investigation.

- Knowledge of the subject matter in question

This is based on the investigator's area of expertise, e.g. having the skills of a forensic accountant as compared to those of a health and safety expert.

Each investigation will therefore have to be approached differently to ensure the best results for a specific workplace, as well as being able to pass muster when put to the test of legal compliance.

Pillar 3. Follow all internal policies and procedures

Best practice principles and procedures must be followed whenever a legally compliant workplace investigation is conducted. This is because each investigation will have unique 'circumstances, issues, dimensions, challenges and outcomes'[4]. Nevertheless, the investigator must still ensure compliance with investigation policy, methodology and relevant laws.

Among the key policies, procedures and guidelines to be complied with at many workplaces will be the organisation's Code of Conduct; the Disciplinary Code and Procedures; Guidelines on Confidentiality and Ethics at Work; the Employee Handbook; Labour Relations Policy as well as the Labour Relations Act. It is based on all these documents that a legally compliant investigation will be conducted. Still, the subject of the investigation will have to be invited to participate in an investigation meeting, using a letter like the one included here.

Letter of Invitation

LETTER inviting Ms Priya Subramani *who is the subject of the investigation.*

Reference/Case Number: FM001/06/2017

PRIVATE AND CONFIDENTIAL

Ms Priya Subramani

Director: Private Banking

BANK OF BABYLON

121 Long Street

Cape Town, 8000

E-mail: priya1@bankofbabylon.co.za

Dear Ms Subramani

INVITATION TO ATTEND INVESTIGATION INTERVIEW

I invite you to attend an interview about the matters I have been appointed to investigate and report on. Without limiting the matters to be discussed at your interview, I anticipate that the key issues to be addressed with you are:

1. Incidents of financial misconduct taking place at your workplace
2. Your explanation for why your name is alluded to as one of the persons involved in financial misconduct
3. What happened at work during March – June 2017 regarding accounts of clients that were defrauded internally

This letter confirms that the interview will be conducted at ____________ (time), on _________________ (date) at

_______________________ (location). It is expected that you set aside ____________ (time period) for this interview.

You are welcome to have a support person or union representative present during the interview. The support person / representative will not be permitted to advocate for you during the interview. However they will be able to observe proceedings, assist with clarifying the process and take notes. The permitted support person / representative must respect the confidentiality of the process. The said support person must not be a witness or person involved in this investigation.

The interview will be electronically recorded, and a copy of the recording will be made available to you upon request. I may also take handwritten notes during the interview.

Please remember that matters which are the subject of the investigation are to remain confidential. This will safeguard the integrity of the process. As such, you are directed not to discuss this matter with colleagues, other employees or any additional person likely to have information relevant to the investigation, other than your support person, union representative or attorney. This directive includes that you do not make comments in relation to this matter on any social media sites.

You are further reminded that your obligations under the Code of Conduct continue to apply throughout and following the conclusion of this process. Failure to meet your obligations about confidentiality may result in disciplinary action being taken against you.

I understand that this may be a difficult time for you and wish to advise that free short term, confidential, face-to-face or telephone counselling is available to all employees through the Employee Assistance Programme, contactable at (021) 487 1248.

If you have any further enquiries about this letter, I can be contacted via email at: mkhuseli3@bankofbabylon.co.za or by telephone at: (021) 487 1200.

Yours sincerely

M. Mankayi (Mr)
Lead Investigator: (Director: Industrial Relations)

Signature: ______________________

Date: __________________________

Pillar 4. Protect against bias

One of the costliest mistakes made by employers when investigating workplace disciplinary matters is to appoint an investigator with vested interests in the outcome. This could be because the investigator has an axe to grind with the employee; or he may seek to curry favour with the employer. Alternatively, he possibly sees the investigation as an opportunity to climb the corporate ladder. Whatever the reason, there is an ulterior motive.

Either way, the biased investigator will be exposed under cross-examination at a labour dispute resolution forum or the Labour Court. As all competent practitioners will know "investigator objectivity is a principal component of a fair investigation.[5]"

Any investigation with a predetermined outcome will discredit an investigator as well as negatively impact the reputation of the employer. Worse still, a biased investigation can cost the employer if a court of law finds that it led to an unfair dismissal. It must therefore be avoided at all costs.

Pillar 5. Gather all relevant information

In all legally compliant workplace investigations, it is very important for the investigator to ensure that they are ready to present a solid case as a witness, when called upon to do so. This means that they must be ready to present testimony at a disciplinary enquiry, an arbitration hearing, or any other labour dispute resolution forum.

Such information could be from different sources, including but not limited to:

- Witness interviews
- Documents
- Workplace searches
- Photographs / videos of the scene
- Review of electronic files
- Surveillance
- Background / credit checks

Pillar 6. Guard confidentiality and privacy [6]

South African labour relations are characterised by duties, rights and responsibilities of the parties to the employment relationship. All investigations must talk to one or all the above workplace issues.

Thus, by discouraging employees from discussing the subject matter of the investigation or the process itself (except with a representative) employers hope to protect the integrity of the process. This approach is necessary also to maintain a level of privacy for the employee while defending the interests of the employer, depending on the circumstances surrounding the investigation.

At the same time, there is no rule which precludes the employer from collecting evidence through electronic communication interception, surveillance techniques, witness statements and documentation. However, this sophisticated activity must be done in compliance with all the applicable legislation including the Protection of Personal Information Act, No. 4 of 2013.

It is important to note that the need for confidentiality begins when a complaint is received, a grievance is laid, or misconduct allegations are made.

Pillar 7. Document preservation and findings [7]

All investigations are legal processes. As such, they must comply with the rule of law. This means that the documents (laws, policies, guidelines) may have to be presented later at a tribunal, an enquiry, a hearing or in a court of law.

Thus, they have to be marked and paginated sequentially as 'exhibits' to be presented as evidence, for it is based on these documents that findings will be made. The documents collected will then be placed in an investigation file.

An investigation case file will be kept separate, but contain the following:

- Investigation Terms of Reference
- Letter of Appointment of the Investigator(s)
- Investigation Plan, with dates for starting and the planned completion
- List of Witnesses to be interviewed, or those who were interviewed
- Applicable policy, guidelines and laws to be reviewed in connection with the subject matter of the investigation
- A Report with only the facts uncovered, issues that could not be proved factually, and investigator's recommendations, which is to be circulated only to the final decision maker

Pillar 8. Protect against retaliation towards complainant or others [8]

As pointed out in the introduction, workplace investigations are of different types. Those that lead to retaliation deal with burning issues such as sexual harassment, victimisation, bullying or scapegoating. In all these cases, it is usually a subordinate "against" his / her superior – a supervisor or manager. The reality of the employment relationship is that it is unequal by design.

Thus, in the context of employment investigations, retaliation occurs when the employer punishes an employee for engaging in a legally protected activity, such as reporting health and safety law compliance lapses to a government agency such as the Inspections and Enforcement Services of the Department of Labour.

The result would be that the whistleblower, thus identified, is then subjected to negative action by the employer. This person then becomes a scapegoat who is victimised by the employer representatives and blamed for anything amiss.

The scapegoat may subsequently be targeted to be demoted for the smallest infraction, receives negative performance reviews, or is dismissed based on a trumped-up list of employment offences. Retaliation can also be subtle, such as management ignoring beneficial inputs made by the employee in meetings or not acknowledging the employee's contribution.

In other instances, the employer might encourage the whistle-blower's colleagues to gang up against the person or transfer them to an undesirable location without following due process. The list of retaliation activities is endless, but they are all illegal conduct because they create a toxic workplace. It is therefore incumbent on an ethical investigator to nip this in the bud as soon as they become aware of it.

One of the techniques an ethical investigator can use is to note the victimisation and report it, when writing the Investigation Report, as an urgent issue to be tackled by the organisation, even if it was not part of the initial terms of reference. The investigator can also recommend the immediate enforcement of an Anti-Retaliation Policy where one is in existence internally.

On the other hand, the investigator can bring this to the attention of the employer as a reputational issue or inform the victimised employee to make use of the Grievance Procedure to ensure that the issues are addressed.

Pillar 9. Follow Up [9]

A workplace investigation is usually an internally generated organisational process. On the other hand it may be a result of a reported violation of national legislation. Thus, administratively, there are many parties involved in the investigation. It is to them that the investigator needs to account after the report is finalised. This means communicating with each party separately, for reasons of confidentiality. To illustrate:

- A letter needs to be written to the person who reported the matter explaining that the investigation is completed, thanking them for reporting the issue, and informing them that a report will be forwarded to the decision makers who appointed the investigator. In addition, assurances that corrective action, if required, will be undertaken speedily.
- The witnesses must also be contacted and advised that the process is completed and that if there is anything else they think can be added as a concern, this would be the time to come forward – before decisions are made.
- Additionally, the decision makers will have to be contacted later by the investigator. This is to check if they have acted on the report's recommendations as part of the way forward, ensuring compliance, and to remind them to inform parties to the investigation by advising them that indeed the matter is closed.
- As part of the way forward, the investigator will have to continue to work with the employer. This will ensure that a culture of ethical conduct is cultivated in order to minimise labour disputes and avoid reputational risks caused by non-compliance with the law, policies, guidelines and collective agreements within the workplace.

Pillar 10. Act [10]

Investigations eventually come to an end. Thus, after the workplace investigation is completed, it is important that the investigator consider recommending what to do in order to integrate systems, processes and procedures to avoid a recurrence of the trigger event, incident or issue.

Recommendations can include any of the items listed below. These should be applied objectively and on a case by case basis:

- A need for conciliation or mediation between the complainant and the subject of the investigation – where alternative dispute resolution is a preferred intervention
- Counselling for the parties – in a sexual harassment case
- A formal apology tendered – if the matter is not serious misconduct
- Training on building a harmonious workplace
- Communication of policies to employees through information sessions
- Disciplinary action, including issuing a warning, demotion, transfer or even dismissal of the perpetrator in a harassment or victimisation case
- Increased supervision or monitoring at the workplace in the interests of harmony
- Disciplinary action taken against the internal complainant if the complaint was frivolous, vexatious or malicious
- Advising a party or parties to appeal if they are not satisfied with the outcome of the investigation [11]

In summary

A legally compliant employment investigation must be conducted through a Workplace Investigation Policy / Protocol that guides the organisation through all the stages of an investigation.

It is based on this document that an employer can demonstrate later that it has followed the rules of natural justice. This includes that, in conformity with procedural fairness requirements, the subject of an investigation was invited in writing to attend an investigation interview and that his duties, rights and responsibilities were outlined in that letter. More importantly, the employer must show that they followed the procedural fairness requirements outlined in the *Code of Good Practice: Dismissal*, step-by-step as described in the pillars above.

Thus, the adverse decision taken by the employer against the employee was not a spur of the moment reaction, but a result of a carefully crafted legal process. Hence the entire process is documented in the Investigation Report prepared by the investigator. The Report details the legal basis for the dismissal of the employee who was charged with gross misconduct, makes it clear that the employee was afforded an opportunity to state a case in defence with the assistance of a representative, appeared at a disciplinary hearing that was procedurally and substantively fair, and was ultimately found guilty.

Template

Model investigation plan

Instruction:

Use this document to plan your investigation. If changes to the information in the plan occur during your investigation, they can be recorded in the Notes column on each page.

1. Investigation overview	Notes
Issue(s) to be investigated: ____________________ ____________________ How the referral was received: ____________________ ____________________ When the referral was received: ____________________ When the case was accepted: ____________________ Investigator assigned: ____________________ Summary of the complaint: ____________________ ____________________ ____________________	Only facts are to be pursued in the investigation. Who __________ When __________ Where __________ Why __________ What was said _____ _______________ _______________ _______________ _______________

Risks to the investigation	Notes
Suspects who are possible flight risks: ____________________ ____________________ Destruction of documents: ____________________ ____________________ Anticipated delays: ____________________ ____________________ Lack of cooperation: ____________________ ____________________ Fear of reprisal: ____________________ ____________________ Collusion between witnesses: ____________________ ____________________ ____________________ Other risks: ____________________ ____________________	Important electronic evidence may be destroyed if handled by an incompetent service provider. It is highly recommended that the Investigator develop a risk management approach to address all the identified risks. Use your words carefully when referring to those involved in the complaint. Stick with neutral language. Avoid words like 'accused' or 'victims' as they can appear to imply a particular conclusion.

Involved parties	Notes
Complainant(s): ____________________ ____________________ Alleged wrongdoer(s): ____________________ ____________________ Witnesses: ____________________ ____________________ Other involved parties / agencies: ____________________ ____________________	

2. Scope of the Investigation	**Notes**
Sources of evidence Documents: ____________________ ____________________ ____________________ Witnesses: ____________________ ____________________	

Expert input: ______________________________ ______________________________ Other sources of information Employee handbook: ______________________________ ______________________________ Applicable laws: ______________________________ ______________________________ ______________________________ Employer policies: ______________________________ ______________________________ Research related to the allegation(s): ______________________________ ______________________________ ______________________________ ______________________________ ______________________________ Areas not being investigated and why: ______________________________ ______________________________ ______________________________	

3. Investigation Steps	Notes
List of activities to be performed Activity: ______________________ ______________________ Person Responsible: Timeframe: ______________________ ______________________ Activity: ______________________ ______________________ Person Responsible: Timeframe: ______________________ ______________________ Activity: ______________________ ______________________ Person Responsible: Timeframe: ______________________ ______________________	Investigation programme could include activities like: • Requesting video footage from an incident location • Reserving a room for investigation interviews • Contacting outside experts for forensic analysis, specialist legal advice, etc. • Making interview appointments • Communicating with the IT Directorate to gather electronic evidence • Reporting allegations of theft; assault; obtaining financial advantage by deception; obtaining property by deception, as well as secret commissions to the SAPS and other law enforcement agencies

Interview plan with locations	Notes
Interview subject: ____________________ ____________________ Location: Date & Time: ____________________ ____________________ Interview subject: ____________________ ____________________ Location: Date & Time: ____________________ ____________________ Interview subject: ____________________ ____________________ Location: Date & Time: ____________________ ____________________	Interviews should be conducted on neutral ground, in a private place. The interview room should have as little as possible distractions and be easily accessible for the interviewee. Choose interview locations carefully.

Document management	Notes
Where will documents be stored? ______________________ ______________________ How will documents be recorded? ______________________ ______________________ Who will have access to them? ______________________ ______________________ Communication plan Who will have access to case information? ______________________ ______________________ Who will have access to specified information? ______________________ ______________________ Who will not have access to case information? ______________________ ______________________ Will law enforcement (SAPS) be involved? ______________________	It is important for all investigators to observe the following information management protocols: • Do not put information documents on an unsecured computer • Do not leave documents on a printer or photocopy machine • Avoid leaving incoming or outgoing faxes on the fax machine • Do not leave investigation messages on desks or phone services • Do not send sensitive material by mail • Refrain from giving confidential information to others to copy, type, address or send

4. Confidentiality	Notes
Media: ________________ ________________ Other employees: ________________ ________________ General public: ________________ ________________ Concerns not covered elsewhere in the plan: ________________ ________________	Standard practice in employment investigations is that employers must not request that employees keep details of an investigation confidential without a legitimate documented reason. This rationale must be explained by filling in this part of the investigation plan.

Adapted: I-Sight: Conducting Workplace Investigations: Step-By-Step

5. Costs and Budgets	Services required? Y/N	Budget Amount
1. Forensic experts		
2. Travel and related costs		
3. Transcription		
4. E-discovery		
5. Legal advice		
6. Translation		
7. Administrative costs		
8. Miscellaneous		

Explanation:

The Investigation Plan must have a timetable for when interviews are to be completed. It should also include a period within the plan for gathering evidence as well as an anticipated time to submit factual findings. This will include a report on what has been proven, while also listing what has not been proved by the investigation. It is also important that a financial plan be done hence the costs and budget table included here.

Chapter 2

Just the Facts

Processes, Systems and Procedures to investigate

"An impartial investigation is generally conducted so that an employer can determine what occurred when there are contested allegations affecting the workplace that can involve a potential violation of the employer's policies, standards, ethics, or the law."

- Guiding Principles for Conducting an Impartial Investigation, Canadian Association of Workplace Investigators

Introduction

Conducting a workplace investigation is a scientific process. It is informed by activities that must be explained based on their results, showing on a balance of probabilities that the outcome is based only on facts. For a suspected employee to be found guilty of misconduct, it must be shown that he contravened one of the following:

1. In terms of the contract of employment of the person being investigated, he is not allowed to bring the employer's name into disrepute by being rude to customers, or by breaching the company's

code of conduct. This code forms part of the terms and conditions of employment of all employees.

2. Employee behaviour is regulated through a disciplinary code and procedure which lists prohibited workplace behaviour. In this regard, disallowed behaviour is known as acts of misconduct.

If an employee is alleged to have breached any of the above legal prescripts or policy guidelines they are accused of an offence. This means that there is a case to be answered, hence the need for an investigation before deciding on the guilt (or otherwise) of the person. The said investigation must then list the rules that have been violated by the offending employee. It must also show, factually, that the rule(s) are reasonable and that they were known to the employee from the day of his Induction training, where it was communicated to him by the employer.

It is standard practice for the employer to enforce the rules through decided cases in the past where offending employees have been charged with misconduct. The same procedure must be followed as was done in previous cases of misconduct in order to avoid inconsistencies.

This then becomes the science of conducting a workplace investigation.

Practice Guide

Workplace Investigation Framework

Investigation overview

- Show how the information came to the employer's attention
- List the specific allegations being investigated
- Write down the general details given by the source
- Show the results of any other initial enquiries
- Explain why the investigation is being conducted (rationale)

Scope and purpose

- As defined by the investigator and approved by the accounting officer (terms of reference)

Resources

- Personnel required (team)
- Expert opinions required
- Technical facilities (audio, video, etc.)
- Mode of transport

Timeframe

- Start time and planned completion

Affected persons

- Employees
- Stakeholders
- Business partners
- Government agencies

Responsibilities

- As per activities table

Risk management

a. Identify possible outcomes
b. Identify core factual issues (in context)
c. Identify investigation activities

- Establish investigation context
- Identify legal, financial, reputational and other risks
- Analyse identified risks
- Evaluate these risks
- Treat risks
- Regular assessment of risks, after drafting the plan, after meeting specific milestones or at critical stages during the investigation

Information gathering tasks

a. Identify potential avenues and sources of information
b. Documents
c. Research reports to be cited

- Documents and items to be collected
- Personal accounts of events and incidents
- Witnesses interviewed or identified to be engaged

Notes:

This framework is an explanation of the investigation plan. It is developed as a theoretical guide explaining how to implement the step-by-step approach developed by the author. It is aligned with the template steps.

More importantly, the purpose of the framework is to show practitioners how to do things differently from what has been standard practice in both the public and private sectors in South Africa. Thus, the same modus operandi will be applied, regardless of the type of investigation being conducted, how the complaint has been received by the employer (hotline, webpage, complaint form or as a grievance) or what the investigation protocol or policy prescribe. It does not matter who is being investigated in the workplace, the investigator must still comply. This ultimately builds consistency of practice in conducting workplace investigations.

The Legal Compliance Imperative[1]

For an employer to convincingly claim to have conducted a procedurally correct workplace investigation, prior to arriving at an adverse decision, it must be able to demonstrate the following compliance aspects:

- The investigation was conducted in order to determine whether enough factual evidence existed to call a disciplinary hearing for misconduct or poor work performance, including a grievance meeting, as the case may be.
- The purpose of the investigation was to collect evidence that could be presented at a hearing, or later at a labour dispute resolution forum, should the matter escalate to that level.
- That the employer had become aware of the allegations of misconduct or an event bringing its name into disrepute. In light of this, the employer would have been duty bound to investigate, as required by acceptable standards for building a decent workplace based on the rule of law and natural justice.

- An employee raised a grievance about the behaviour of a colleague or supervisor / manager such as sexual harassment, victimisation, bullying or any other prohibited behaviour; and that, therefore, the organisation was required to investigate if it was to avoid being cited as second respondent in the dispute.
- Even though there was no compulsion to investigate instances of misconduct, it was advisable that an investigation be conducted as it appeared on face value that there was a likelihood of a dismissal occurring.

Tactically, given all the above points of law, it is clearly advisable to conduct an investigation in order to satisfy the requirement for procedural fairness, as provided for in Item 4 (1) of the *Code of Good Practice: Dismissal*, in Schedule 8 of the Labour Relations Act, 66 of 1995.

More importantly, it is also advisable to investigate in order to show that the employer is not complicit in any acts of illegality (sexual harassment, victimisation or bullying cases). In this way, the alleged victim cannot claim vicarious liability on the part of the employer, as long as the employer can show that it intervened by taking a complaint seriously, advised the employee of the available options to address toxic workplace behaviour and can confidently show which actions it took when the matter was brought to its attention.

Conducting the Investigation[2]

This aspect of the process is essentially a fact-finding exercise. The intended outcome is based on the scope of the investigation, as agreed between the employer and the investigator. The investigator may be someone internal or an externally hired person. Such terms of reference, as they are listed, will talk to issues including:

- The reasons for convening an investigation, which may be the result of whistle blower allegations, a complaint by a manager or a fellow employee, an enquiry by a regulatory authority or a prompt by a government department with jurisdiction to raise pertinent issues.
- Defining the authority empowered to initiate the investigation. Done according to the delegated powers in the relevant governance document of the employer, empowering a board of directors, an audit committee, the executive authority, or accounting officer to whom the investigator should report after completing the investigation.
- The same scope of investigation will give a directive to the investigator to preserve relevant data for accountability purposes as well as to maintain confidentiality.
- As part of the terms of reference, the investigator will be given powers to interview employees who may have relevant information.
- The investigator is informed as to whom a report will have to be delivered to, in writing or during a meeting, and where it is to be presented. All of this depends on the constitution of the employer or any other prescript.
- The types of investigations that can be undertaken in that workplace. In addition to HRM issues like misconduct and job performance, these could also include harassment, discrimination allegations, disability management and Compensation for Occupational Injuries and Diseases Act (COIDA) issues. Internal Audit queries relating to compliance with policies, processes and procedures to mitigate employment risks can also be included here.
- Additional types of investigations that relate to matters between staff and customers as well as criminal wrongdoing, including corruption and theft.

Practice Guide

Workplace investigation methodology

The Investigator(s) are hereby delegated to undertake any reasonable and legal activity associated with the gathering of all facts and information relevant to this investigation. Such activities could include, but are not restricted to, the use of the following procedures:

- Access, obtain, retrieve and copy all records considered relevant to finding out the facts relevant to the allegations.

- Attend and inspect all relevant employer facilities and/or premises.

- Make reasonable attempts to access any other evidence (not held by the employer) which is considered relevant to these allegations.

- Give appropriate lawful directions which may be required during this investigation, e.g. keep the investigation confidential, attend an interview or provide copies of relevant documents.

- Conduct interviews with persons who can contribute information relevant to the investigation through the relevant line manager or HRM department.

- Seek to conduct interviews with relevant persons who are not employees of the organisation.

Determine who should Investigate[3]

It has already been noted earlier that there are different types of workplace investigations. All of them will be informed by the legal and policy context applicable to the issues at hand as well as to the situation on the ground. This includes the levels of unionisation, or a lack of unionisation. It is this preliminary analysis that will indicate to the employer what type of person(s) to appoint as an investigator.

In addition, while determining who should investigate, it might be decided that a specific matter or issue will be investigated by an external professional, or an outside specialist. This is usually the case where there is the potential for protracted litigation, such as; fraud, corruption, violations of public and social policy guidelines, national legislation, or a matter of national interest.

With respect to general workplace issues, including misconduct or job performance investigations, the employer can use internal HRM/ER personnel. This includes health and safety professionals, IT staff, security officials, internal auditors or in-house legal advisors, depending on the nature of the employer's operations.

More importantly, internal investigators, without exception, must be able to demonstrate the following traits:

- Neutrality:

  Notwithstanding the fact that they are appointed by the employer.

- Expertise:

  If it is a matter relating to financial misconduct, a professional accountant, or a law professional with forensic capability, may have to be appointed instead of a generalist practitioner.

- Credibility:

  The investigator should not be tainted by an association with any of the parties involved in the investigation – directly or indirectly.

- Availability:

  The investigation should not be drawn out unnecessarily as a result of conflicts between the investigator's schedule and the plans of the employer

Practice Guide

Selection an investigation team

In order to be selected for the investigation team a candidate should:

- Possess the ability to understand the purpose of the investigation.
- Grasp the business impact of the investigation.
- Have a good fit between the communication style of the interviewer and the interviewee.
- Have experience independence from the objects of the investigation.
- Be able to perform effectively as a potential witness.
- Be able to keep matters pertaining to the investigation privileged.
- Be able to maintain confidentiality.
- Possess good writing skills.
- Be proficient in professional speaking.
- Have enough experience and skill in workplace investigations.
- Have enough expertise in the subject matter of the investigation to understand the issues and know what information is needed to fully address all the relevant issues.
- Have the necessary resources and available time to play a role.

Get the complaint in writing

Some issues requiring a workplace investigation, both in the private sector and public service, are reported anonymously through a hot line. An example of this could be a customer alleging that employees ask for bribes in order to deliver certain public services or to give them access to SMME business opportunities. Difficult as this situation is, it is advisable that an employer make an effort to get to the bottom of the allegations, in order to avoid being accused of dereliction of duty. If it is discovered that it was a baseless allegation the matter can then be laid to rest. However, if there is a case to be made the matter should be pursued.

Conduct the investigation promptly[4]

PSCBC Resolution 1 of 2003[5], which regulates employee relations in South Africa's public sector, is silent on this issue. As a result, there are no time frames or guidelines advising the State, as employer, regarding when to start and potentially complete an investigation resulting in the dismissal of an employee, as provided for under Item 4 (1) of the *Code of Good Practice: Dismissal.* Furthermore, none of the many public sector bargaining councils have an investigation methodology or a protocol to assist employers within their jurisdiction regarding the conduct of a workplace investigation. Yet the PSC has investigation guidelines[6].

The issue of an investigation only arises in relation to a 'precautionary suspension' of an employee who is charged with serious misconduct. This is either an omission on the part of the negotiators who concluded this collective agreement or a strategic decision that was taken by the parties, with specific intent. Whichever way one looks at it, this is a risk that needs to be managed by the employer. Still, it is my submission that this situation can be corrected by amending the disciplinary code and procedures for the public service. In practice, this means stipulating a time period within which to start and complete an investigation in order to minimise the risk of disputes.

The purpose is to ensure that there is certainty about what is to be done in order to comply with the maxim which says that "justice delayed is justice denied". The practice in the public service, currently, is that an employee is charged with gross misconduct without any necessary legally compliant investigation having been conducted. In my view, the PSCBC is the appropriate forum to address this matter as it represents the public sector.

On the other hand, in the private sector guidelines relating to conducting a workplace investigation may be dependent on the standard practice in that sector or industry. This includes legal guidelines as per collective agreements or corporate governance documents, including any applicable policy for each employer. As a result, the situation varies from one context to another. Again, none of the sector specific collective agreements negotiated at the various bargaining councils give the necessary guidance to employers on how to timeously conduct an investigation. This is another best practice gap that needs to be filled in order to standardise employee relations management from agriculture, manufacturing, mining, all the way to the services industry. Here sector employer organisations are key.

It will be difficult to hold any employee accountable if there is insufficient proof to point to wrongdoing. Thus, it is imperative to have a written complaint, to prove that the issues complained about are real and not spurious.

It is therefore advisable that, where possible, the employer insists that the complaint be reduced to a statement, a letter, an affidavit or a designed form. This is helpful in reporting on what was investigated, including the findings emanating from the investigation, so that a decision can be made on what to do to correct a deviation from acceptable behaviour.

Consider an administrative suspension

In situations where it is alleged that an employee or executive has committed gross misconduct (such as fighting at work; victimising workers based on their religion, culture or ideology; or stealing systematically as part of a syndicate of criminals) it may be necessary to suspend such an employee with pay.

Such a suspension is to be explained by the employer as precautionary, not a disciplinary action arising out of a determination of guilt in a disciplinary hearing. This is important in order to protect both the reputation of the organisation as well as the professional image of the employee under suspicion.

In light of this, the internal communication to colleagues and other interested parties must include an explanation to the effect that the administrative suspension is intended to:

- Ensure that there is no interference with the investigation.
- Last for a short period of time and that the parties involved will receive full pay.
- Be executed in good faith, with the intention to act fairly.
- Include the appointment, in the case of executives, of an employee in an acting capacity.

In summary

To the extent that an investigation is a scientific process that follows a legal step-by-step logic, the employer must be able show that the results can be traced by referencing the collected facts. Such facts must further show what was said by the respective parties during interviews, in their own words.

As a result, the investigator can state which of the allegations were not substantiated and which ones were, including which witnesses were credible based on objective criteria. The investigation framework plays a key role in compliance with best practice, as it guides the employer through the issues that need to be covered. As an operational tool it is proof that the investigation was conducted out of a need to see justice served.

Furthermore, the scientific aspect of the investigation must prove to observers that the employer had a clear idea of the scope and purpose of the investigation. Strategically, it must provide a record of how the investigation was conducted, state who performed each role as per the table of activities and explain the methodology used in order to show compliance with processes and procedures. Also as part of the scientific process, the investigation report must show that, while managing the employment relationship, administrative issues such as suspensions were considered, especially when taking into consideration the gravity of the allegations.

Essential characteristics of a competent investigator

- Investigator's experience in conducting workplace investigations
- Investigator's familiarity with the organisation's business or industry including policies, laws and standard operating procedures
- Investigator's professionalism
- Availability of Investigator to execute process timeously
- Credibility and ability to effectively communicate either verbally or in writing regarding findings or as a witness in legal proceedings
- Professional reputation and knowledge about the relevant issues
- Ability to interview witnesses using relevant techniques
- Intellectual ability to conceptualise, design and execute an investigation with various personalities and in varied situations
- Ability to maintain confidentiality to the extent that the law allows

Box 1

Chapter 3

Legal Basis for an Investigation

Legal compliance. Conducting a flawless process

"The code requires employers to investigate reported cases of misconduct to determine whether there may be grounds for dismissal. [...] A pre-hearing investigation is precisely what its name suggests. During this phase, the employer investigates the alleged offence in order to decide whether formal disciplinary action may be justified. This will normally entail interviewing witnesses, including possibly the employee concerned, and inspecting relevant documents."

- John Grogan, Dismissal[1]

Introduction

The difference between a workplace disciplinary process based on the rule of law and an action taken by the 'rule of the mob' is that the former is characterised by a search for justice, whilst the latter is about an exercise of power based on a whim. This generally happens in the broader society, as well as in workplaces. South African history is littered with cases where employees were dismissed because their bosses did not like the language they spoke, the religions they belonged to, or their places of origin. To amplify the point, in William Shakespeare's *Julius Caesar*, there is a scene where the mob, after the killing of the main character is baying for blood when one of the poets, Sina, appears. The mob then suggests that Sina be killed, without any proof that he was involved in the conspiracy to kill Julius Caesar, simply because he shares a name with the accused person. By their reasoning, if that is not a satisfactory explanation or reason to charge him with conspiracy to commit murder against Julius Caesar, their hero, then Sina the poet has to be killed for the 'bad verses' in his poetry. This mob-like approach to justice reminds one of cases where workers are dismissed based on trumped-up charges. These charges are usually brought against them merely because they are not part of the inner circle that worships at the altar of the organisation's leadership, or because they do not belong to a certain union.

In such instances the victimised employees will be faced with a 'charge sheet' as long as your arm. Also, in most cases there will be no proof that an investigation was conducted by the employer before arriving at a decision to charge the employee with gross misconduct – a dismissible offence. The absence of a legitimate investigation before a dismissal renders the decision suspect and the employer open to accusations of malpractice.

The South African legislature sought to correct situations like the abovementioned when it introduced a requirement forcing the employer to investigate prior to dismissal. This procedure is to be followed if the employer wishes to pass the test of procedural fairness in employment matters, especially with misconduct allegations[2]. There is an expression in legal matters that says; "the one who alleges must prove". The same principle applies here.

Regulatory and Compliance Framework

In the first chapter, it was noted that there are specific instances that require a legally compliant workplace investigation to be conducted in order to minimise the risk of employment disputes that may result from a failure to comply with legal prescripts.

This analysis is now confirmed by an article in a Bowman Attorneys publication where it is stated: *"The Code of Good Practice: Dismissal* (Schedule 8 of the Labour Relations Act, 66 of 1995) recommends that an investigation be undertaken by an employer to establish if there are grounds for misconduct that may warrant dismissal[3]."

Given the above article, the law is clear on the responsibilities of the employer. The next question relates to how a legally compliant investigation is conducted.

Here is a simple framework that can be applied to the process:

A. When investigating allegations of general misconduct, there are specific activities to be undertaken, including the following:

   1. Seek to obtain just the facts, as shown by a preliminary determination of the issues involved. This includes matters such as a violation of the code of conduct, breach of the disciplinary code, a failure to comply with organisational policy relating to standard work rules, and so forth.
   2. Analytically categorise the issues as serious or gross misconduct, as provided for in the disciplinary code and procedures, or employee handbook.
   3. Decide whether or not the issue could be dealt with through a progressive disciplinary process of warnings to correct deviant behaviour, without having to resort to a disciplinary hearing.
   4. Decide if it is a disciplinary matter that can be investigated internally, or whether or not it must be investigated externally

due to the complex issues involved, the seniority of the affected person, or the identified risks to the organisation.

5. Taking into account the risks involved, decide if it is necessary to suspend the employee on a precautionary basis, pending the outcome of the investigation.
6. Identify potential witnesses, based on the preliminary analysis of the issues identified as potential acts of misconduct and the persons involved.
7. List the documents available as evidence to support the employer's *prima facie* case of misconduct, as well as where they are located.

Only when the employer can satisfactorily tick all the above items off the list can it be decided that there is indeed a case of misconduct to be brought against the alleged perpetrator and that it is winnable. In the absence of the features listed above, the inevitable conclusion would be that the matter cannot proceed.

B. When investigating grievances raised by employees it is also necessary for the HR/ER practitioner to know both the legal and organisational position of the employer when handling workplace grievances. These will normally be contained in collective bargaining agreements that have been negotiated between the employer and a recognised trade union(s). For instance, in the public service in South Africa, most issues that cause grievances, as reported by the PSC[4], relate to promotion, job grading, and performance management.

On the other hand, in the private sector, workplace issues causing grievances usually relate to the interpretation of conditions of employment (contractual), pay and benefits, changing work practices, alleged discrimination, bullying and harassment, health and safety issues, promotion and grading, as well as issues with fellow employees[5]. The above two lists are neither exclusive to a sector, nor exhaustive.

The starting point then, when investigating workplace grievances, is to know what constitutes a grievance – defined as dissatisfaction with terms and conditions of employment, or the work environment. Therefore, it must be differentiated from a disciplinary matter appeal, as employees tend to confuse the two in some cases. Following thereon, it is important for a practitioner to be armed with a tool such as the grievance policy and procedure of a specific employer or workplace. This helps when the employer is confronted by an employee who raises a complaint that is based on an opinion or a supposition (an assumption or an emotional reaction), minus the facts that determine it as a workplace grievance.

The basics of investigating a workplace grievance include the following issues (to be handled dialectically):

- If possible, seek to handle the matter informally, as a first step.
- Advise the aggrieved employee that the matter is to be investigated as per the applicable grievance rules, policy and procedure of the company / organisation.
- Undertake to refer the matter to the decision makers at the appropriate level to ensure compliance with the procedure, if applicable.
- Advise the employee that the matter can be escalated to a higher level, after the investigation is completed, if there is dissatisfaction with the outcome. This could be to an internal appeal authority or externally to a competent labour dispute resolution forum.
- Seek at all times to comply with time limits as per procedure or rules.
- The investigator should keep meticulous records in case the matter goes to an external dispute resolution forum, in order to prove the employer's bona fides.

An additional matter that requires investigation by the employer is allegations of poor work performance brought against an employee. In many instances employers confuse the symptoms of inadequate job performance with misconduct.

When identifying poor work performance, is important to consider the following:

- Is there a written performance agreement between the employee and the employer / organisation that can be used to substantiate the claim?
- What is the guidance from the performance management system of the organisation? What is the policy or legal point of view?
- What is the standard practice in dealing with alleged unsatisfactory work performance as claimed by the manager?
- Is this a case of poor work performance due to injury on duty, ill health or a skills gap? Or, is it a case of negligence or even recklessness?

The purpose of asking all the above questions during the investigation is to establish the underlying causes for the alleged poor work performance. The intention is for the employer to determine a way forward based on the applicable laws, organisational policy, and good practice in that industry or sector. The reasoning is that unsatisfactory performance is generally not the fault of the employee. Studies have revealed that many factors may contribute to allegations of unsatisfactory work performance, including the following:

- A lack of competency / training, no requisite qualifications, or lack of experience (needed in order to perform optimally).
- Alcohol or drug addiction as a result of domestic challenges.
- Outside influences (long standing disputes with employer).

- Work related stress as a result of alleged unfair labour practices.
- Incompatibility with the organisational culture or managementstyle[6].

International research has further shown that the above issues can be addressed by an employer, through recommendations of an investigator that show:

- How to manage employee performance.
- Why managing performance is important to an employer.
- How a performance management system can be developed and introduced (where it does not exist).
- How to plan employee performance / manage underperformance.
- What is involved in performance reviews[7].

Framework for general workplace misconduct investigations

1. Employer's responsibilities
   (As per Item 4 (1) and (4) of the *Code of Good Practice: Dismissal*, Schedule 8 of the LRA, 66 of 1995)
2. The identified investigator's role
3. How to collect evidence (applying rules and law of evidence)
4. How to interview witnesses and take statements from them
5. How to record and prepare witness statements
6. How to prepare and structure an investigation report
7. What to do after you have prepared the report
8. Keeping an investigation file

***Box 2:** Adapted from Mike Totten's 'Workplace Investigations: The Do's and Don'ts, in Workplace Info, 29 January 2016.*

Getting it right the first time

The subtitle of this book is 'Minimising the Risk of Labour Law Disputes'. By definition, a risk is explained as 'uncertainty as to the outcome of an event when two or more possibilities exist[8]'. True to the application of this definition is an unfair dismissal caused by a failure to investigate the facts connected to the event / occurrence that triggered the events leading up to the dismissal. It is a very costly risk to take as the remedies for an unfair dismissal can go up to twelve months of compensation paid out to the employee for an ordinary dismissal, or even twenty four months for an automatically unfair dismissal. Therefore it is essential for an employer to get it right from the beginning, especially if the goal is to avoid cases where employees declare disputes. These disputes will be referred to the bargaining councils or to the CCMA and, ultimately, end up at the labour court where there is a greater possibility that the ruling will favour the employee.

In practice this means that the employer must put in place policy guidelines, operational processes and implementation systems (professional practice guides) to ensure that employees will accept detrimental organisational decisions taken against them by the employer, so long as they can see that justice has been done.

This will be addressed in the following section by showing employers and workplace practitioners how to do things differently.

A. Right to representation during a workplace investigation

South African employment law, specifically the LRA, 66 of 1995, is silent on whether an accused employee can be accompanied to an investigation.

Instead, the right to representation is accorded to employees when they are called to a disciplinary hearing. This is permitted on the basis that there is a provision for this right in negotiated disciplinary procedures in unionised workplaces. This right is then brought up and the option of representation offered when a notice to appear in a disciplinary hearing is forwarded to the affected employee, but very rarely when an employee is to be interviewed by an investigator.

Normally, the right to representation during a workplace investigation is not regarded as standard employment relations practice in the private sector or the public service. However, it is good practice for the employer to allow an employee to be represented or to be accompanied by a colleague, if it is requested. The objective is to avoid an instance where a trade union can allege that the employer interfered with the right to fair procedure when the employee requested accompaniment or representation.

Furthermore, the case law is not sufficiently conclusive when it comes to the authority on this matter. Thus, employees can be accompanied by a colleague or shop steward to confer with from time to time. The understanding being that all the questions posed to the affected person will be answered by the employee who is the subject of the investigation. Thus, the role of the companion will be merely to observe the process.

B. Right of an employee to refuse to answer questions as opposed to the right of the employer to demand answers

It has been noted in a previous chapter that access to justice at work is a constitutional imperative. It is therefore guaranteed as a human right for all citizens, as per section 23 of the Constitution of the Republic, Act

108 of 1996. Hence the dictum, "everyone is presumed innocent, until proven guilty".

More importantly, the issues addressed in this section refer to events, incidents and occurrences under review in the course of the employment relationship, between the employer and the employee. In this respect, it is important to remember that such an employment relationship is regulated by law, public and social policy, organisational prescripts, a contract of employment, as well as good practice in a given sector or industry in South Africa. Moreover, all the above instruments talk to the rights, duties and responsibilities of the employer and the employee at work.

The right of an employee to refuse to answer questions posed in a workplace investigation depends on the questions being asked by the employer. It is important to note that this right is not absolute. An employee is duty bound to answer all the questions posed by the investigator, who has been appointed by the employer in order to determine findings of fact, as well as to decide on the credibility of the employee as a witness. In other words, no avoidance is allowed if the investigation is legitimately undertaken by the employer in order to protect its business interests. For the rule of law to prevail employees are required to answer all questions.

Of equal importance here is the employee's duty to cooperate in the workplace, as well as to truthfully provide management with information when so instructed. As a rule of thumb, failure to cooperate can lead to a charge of insubordination (a dismissible offence) depending on the issues being investigated. The duty of the employee to cooperate does not grant the employer the right to interrogate an employee. However, the employee has a contractual obligation to assist the employer in discovering the facts relating to a situation that potentially casts an employee as a wrongdoer. This distinction is critical.

An exception must be made where the possibility of criminal

prosecution arises and the employee feels that they may incriminate themselves by answering questions.

The right to remain silent arises only in situations where the questions posed by the investigator during the interview do not relate to performance of the employee's official duties. The employee can refuse to answer these questions if there is possible self-incrimination. In this instance, the employer can then decide to suspend the employee pending the outcome of the workplace investigation. This situation may encourage the employer to add a further charge of insubordination to the ones being contemplated, if they so wish, in spite of the risk. If the employee raises the issue of legal safeguards against a possibility of criminal self-incrimination, it is advisable that an employer present a form dealing with this matter, as an organisational tool[9].

This form must include a signed declaration acknowledging that the administrative advisement has been given to the employee, informing him of his rights in relation to the questions to be asked regarding issues outside of the scope of his employment. The employee can sign the form voluntarily, in the presence of his representative and the person (investigator) giving the administrative advisement. This form must then be witnessed and dated by all present. This is for the employer to avoid being accused of coercing the employee to cooperate, as an alternative to dismissal or the threat of imprisonment.

In order to avoid this difficult situation, it is also advisable that during the investigation the employer asks questions specifically, directly and narrowly relating to the employee's performance of official duties. The employee can be dismissed based on his answers, or for refusing to answer legitimate questions during the investigation. Again, this is dependent on the employer being able to properly discharge their duty in order to prove that, on the balance of probability, the employee has a *prima facie* case of misconduct to answer to.

It must be remembered that the investigation is an opportunity for the employee to be heard, as required by the *audi alterem partem* principle (meaning, to listen to the other side). Any failure to exercise this right can be fatal for the employee's case in a disciplinary hearing. If the employee does not capitalise on the opportunity to have their side of the matter heard there will only be the employer's version of events to go on in the event of a dispute.

A suggested format for the employer's line of questioning (relating to the above) is included here as an illustration. Admittedly, this is a novel approach to dealing with the issues under consideration. Nevertheless, the intention is to promote access to justice for both the employer and employee during a workplace investigation.

DUTY TO COOPERATE ADVISEMENT FORM

Location: Tsonga Municipality Date: 3/04/2016
Time: 09:00 am

---

1. I wish to advise you that you are being questioned as part of an official investigation by the City of Tsonga (EMS) Division (employer).
2. You will be asked questions specifically and narrowly related to the performance of your official duties and responsibilities or fitness to hold office.
3. You are entitled to all the rights and privileges guaranteed by the laws of the country and the Constitution of the Republic of South Africa, Act 108 of 1996, including the right not to be compelled to incriminate yourself.
4. I further wish to advise you that if you refuse to testify or refuse to answer questions relating to the performance of your official duties and responsibilities, or fitness for duty, you will be subject to departmental charges, which could result in dismissal from employment with the City of Tsonga (EMS) Division.
5. If you do answer, neither your statements nor any information or evidence which is gained by reason of such statements can be used against you in any subsequent criminal proceedings. These statements, however, may be used against you in relation to subsequent departmental charges.

I, K.T. Magama, Persal No: ____________________, hereby declare that I have been given the administrative advisement form by the employer investigator, Mr.____________________ during the investigation interview held as above.

Signature: ____________________________

Date: _______________________________

Witnesses:

1. ________________________________ (Name and Surname)

Signature: _______________________ (Employee Representative)

2. ________________________________ (Name and Surname)

Signature: _______________________ (Employer Representative)

____

____

Adapted from Employee Refusal to Cooperate in Internal Investigations: Into the Woods with Employers, Courts and Labor Arbitrators, Marian F. Hill, Jr. & James A. Wright, Missouri Law Review, Volume 56, 1991.

C. Privileged Information[10]

During workplace investigations it happens that an investigator interviews an affected employee (investigation subject) about an event, incident or occurrence to establish the facts, only to be told that the question cannot be answered because it veers towards what is known as privileged information. This is normally an interpretation of a legal principle known as lawyer-client privilege. Analytically, there are different types of privileged information in workplace investigations, including:

1. A discussion between an affected person or aggrieved employee and his union representative as it relates to their legal approach to handling the matter at hand. This includes the documents they will use to state their case.
2. Labour relations communications between a supervisor/manager and the employers' labour relations practitioners as they constitute legal advice.
3. Consultations between in-house counsel and external counsel on the one hand, and executive management of the employer organisation on the other, on the legal approach to handling a sexual harassment lawsuit brought against the employer by an employee.

Regardless of the parties involved in a legal discussion as a result of the workplace investigation underway, information relating to legal advice on how to institute or defend a matter is privileged and cannot be divulged to the opposite party. This rule does not apply to facts relating to the legal advice.

Thus, in determining what privileged information is, it is important to note that this relates to:

- A communication between a client and "legal practitioner", as defined in the LRA[11].
- Discussions held in confidence for the purpose of obtaining legal advice.
- A work product (advice document) in anticipation of a workplace dispute, external forum litigation, or a trial in a court of law.

Any other information arising out of a workplace investigation can be disclosed at a workplace meeting such as a grievance / disciplinary hearing or at a dispute meeting upon showing good cause by the applicant, as to why it is necessary to have access to such a document or evidence in the possession of the other party.

D. Employee Rights during a workplace investigation

The following items need to be taken into account:

1. If HRM/ER practitioners request the presence of an employee who is the subject of an investigation at an investigation meeting, the employee has the right to ask and be informed of the general subject of the investigation.
2. If the employer fails to respond to the request for information, the employee is entitled to file a grievance relating to the unfair treatment by the employer, using the grievance procedure.
3. If the employer advises the employee of the possibility of criminal charges being laid as a result of the allegations of misconduct, the employee is permitted to ask for an opportunity to consult with a legal practitioner of their choice, at a reasonable time.
4. The accused employee has the right to insist that only one question

at a time be asked. The employee can also object to repetitious, confusing or unclear questions.

5. Additionally, if the employer refuses to allow the employee to confer with a representative, the employee has the right to request that such a denial be noted for the record including the time, name and job title of the employer representative making the denial decision.
6. The employee has the right to take notes of the questions asked and answers given during the investigation.
7. Where the employer or its representative attempts to intimidate the employee as a witness, the employee can note on the record that a grievance will be lodged, or a dispute declared, concerning the investigation.
8. The employee further has the right to note how the minutes of the investigation are being taken, i.e. shorthand, tape recorder or stenographer.
9. Following the investigation, the employee is further advised not to discuss the issues that are the subject of the investigation with their colleagues, but only with a legal representative.

In summary

This chapter argues for a correct interpretation and application of the *Fair Procedure* section of the *Code of Good Practice: Dismissal.* As such, it recommends that the investigator follows a step-by-step compliance procedure in order to protect the employer, in the event that a dismissal is challenged by an employee as being procedurally and substantively unfair.

In a nutshell, the employer is required to be legally compliant as well as apply international best practice. A time may come when the employer will be required to explain its decision by showing just cause as to how and why an employee was dismissed during an internal disciplinary hearing. Analytically though, the critical issue to note as a practitioner is that there exists both what is required by the law, as well as the need to do what is right as an employer.

It can be deduced that the ultimate purpose of conducting a legally compliant workplace investigation is not to build a case, as many employers tend to do. Rather the purpose of the process is to investigate allegations of misconduct in order to decide whether 'formal disciplinary action may be justified', given the facts uncovered by the investigator. Guided by the appropriate employment relations governance documents such as a disciplinary code and procedures, an employee handbook, relevant case law relating to that matter or an investigation protocol, it will be easy for an employer to take a holistic approach and come to the right decision.

Practice Guide

CHECKLIST FOR MANAGING THE INVESTIGATION PROCESS

Step 1: Pre-complaint

- The employer should ensure all critical organisational policies are in place (including investigation protocol).
- Ensure that HR personnel and managers are properly trained on how to address internal complaints from employees and third parties.

Step 2: After a complaint is lodged

- Identify issues to be investigated.
- Determine who should be advised of the complaint.
- Agree who will be appointed as investigator.
- Consider the implications of union involvement if the workplace is unionised.
- Determine whether the investigation should be attorney-client privileged.
- Plan the timetable for the start and completion of the investigation.
- Consider interim measures (administrative suspension).
- Identify pertinent documents to preserve, including electronic evidence acquisition.

Step 3: Managing the investigation

- Preserve privilege as to communication with all parties.
- Set parameters for the investigation through terms of reference (do not micro-manage investigator).

Step 4: Special issues involving alleged executive misconduct

- Determine whether the investigation should be managed at a Board of Directors' level, rather than by CEO or HRM.
- Consider indemnification / legal representation issues.
- Determine whether executive council will be permitted to participate in investigation interview. If so, define the parameters of such participation.
- Preserve privilege given the risks involved in executive misconduct.
- Implement interim measures (suspension, reassignment, etc.) as per contract of employment.
- Involve law enforcement if criminal conduct is suspected.

Step 5: Conclusion of the investigation

- Communicate with all participants about investigator's findings and conclusions, possible disciplinary action and next steps, all while preserving privilege.
- Manage communications to protect the credibility of process.
- Keep investigations files containing all the necessary documents for a legally acceptable period.
- Ensure that management periodically follows up to ensure no retaliation, further harassment or victimisation of any person occurs.
- For executives accused of misconduct, carefully analyse severance provisions in contracts of employment in order to ensure compliance.

Box 3: *Adapted from Michael, L. Rosen's "Workplace Investigations: Checklist for Management Attorneys". American Bar Association Presentation for Contracts and Executive Compensation Subcommittee, 23 March 2017.*

Section B

Building the Structure

Chapter 4

Organisational Preparation

Procedural Fairness. Getting the facts straight
Applying the AUDI Principle

"Effective and appropriate workplace investigations might insulate an employer from liability for an adverse employment action – even if the investigation yields a personnel decision based on a mistaken fact. [...] A reasonable (not just good faith) investigation will dictate whether an employer has acted reasonably."

- American Bar Association: Workplace Investigations

Introduction

A legally compliant workplace investigation is a step-by-step process[1] that can be appreciated by an objective observer. As part of this process, measures need to be taken so the employer is able to systematically show that it never had any ulterior motives. Also, it should be made clear that the employer's management team is determined to apply its organisational mind. This is done by demonstrating a clear and transparent planning process. It must be shown that the investigation will include a review of evidentiary documents, as well as the interviewing of witnesses, in order to get only the facts and evidence relating to the issues that triggered the investigation. This level of thoroughness can be explained in terms of the following activities:

1. On receiving a complaint / allegation

   It is widely accepted that many organisations have policy guidelines on the management of the employment relationship. This usually includes matters that can lead to the termination of the employee's contract of employment by the employer, when just cause is shown. When the employer receives a complaint relating to an alleged violation of a Code of Conduct, a policy or procedure, the employer will have to decide if an investigation is necessary based on the assessment of preliminary issues. This assessment includes listing the policies and guidelines that will have to be referenced. The objective is to determine whether the complaint is trivial, frivolous or vexatious[2]. Once the employer has clarity on the nature of the complaint, it will then appoint an investigator to attend to the matter. This activity is undertaken to prove that 'procedural fairness is the yardstick by which [the] employer's pre-dismissal actions are measured'[3]. In compliance with best practice, the employer is also required to check that the allegations are within the required timeframe for raising a complaint or grievance.

2. After a complaint is registered

   The investigation manager is required to draft terms of reference, to be approved by the employer, outlining the issues to be investigated based on a complaint letter received or a grievance form submitted to the organisation.

   At the same time the leadership (in the form of an accounting officer and/or the appointed investigator) must determine who should be advised of the complaint. The protocol document is carefully consulted before commencing an internal investigation and based on its prescripts and recommended actions, an investigation plan is then developed.

In a unionised workplace that has a collective agreement as one of the employment relations governance documents, it is advisable that the employer inform the union in writing that a member (and especially a shop steward) is the subject of an investigation. This action is simply a courtesy, but it is also intended to avoid accusations of non-compliance with a workplace collective agreement.

As an integral part of the investigation plan, the investigation manager must plan the commencement and probable completion dates of the investigation. A table of activities approved by the organisation should be included in the investigation plan and this will drive the process forward.

It is considered the rule of thumb to keep confidential the decision by the employer to investigate any allegations of breach of policy, law, codes or rules. Such an investigation must also comply with the rules of natural justice, rules of evidence, the 'balance of probabilities' standard of proof, and procedural fairness requirements.

Finally, it is important to remember that the purpose of the terms of reference for the investigation is not to micro-manage the investigation process, or the investigator. The intention is to ensure that the organisation can effortlessly account for every step of the process at a later stage. Especially in the event that there is a legal challenge regarding what prompted the investigation. The responsibility for drafting the terms of reference should rest with the accounting officer, as the key employer representative. Alternatively, the responsibility will rest with a committee of the board of an organisation, or the investigation manager, depending on the governance document or policy of the employer.

Letter informing affected employee s/he is subject of an investigation

Date: ______________________

Dear: ______________________

I am writing to inform you that the organisation has decided to conduct an investigation into your actions, allegedly relating to:

- Corruption by abuse of your position as GM: Corporate Services of Asambe Carriers.
- Victimisation of subordinates who uphold the Code of Conduct of the company as well as the SCM policy.
- Cronyism at the organisation where unqualified persons are appointed.

The person in charge of the investigation will be __________ (Name of investigator) The aim of the investigation is to seek to verify the allegations by gathering as many facts and pieces of information as possible. It is currently expected that the investigation will be completed by ________date / month / year.

Once the investigation is completed you will be informed in writing of its outcome. If it is found that there is a case to answer, you will be advised to attend a disciplinary hearing. The investigator may advise you to attend an investigation meeting where you can explain your version of events. If this is required, you will be informed of the time and date of such a meeting in advance.

In the meantime, should you have any information that might be of assistance in the investigation, or wish to discuss anything, please do not hesitate to contact ___________________ (Name of investigator / line manager / HR department) Their contact details are: ____

(Telephone number / e-mail address / physical address)

To ensure that the investigation can be concluded as fairly as possible, we request that you keep the matter confidential. Any breach of confidentiality may be considered a disciplinary matter.

Please note that you should continue to attend work while the investigation takes place (amend if the suspension of the affected person was necessary).

Furthermore, if you are of the opinion that the company has no legal or factual basis to conduct this workplace investigation, please let us know within forty eight (48) hours of having received this letter.

Yours sincerely

Vijay Prabhakaran

Signature: __________________________

Designation: CEO

Identify a list of activities to be performed

Conducting a workplace investigation is as much a science as an art. This includes carefully balancing the participation of people as witnesses on the one side, listing of evidentiary documents to be used on the other, and managing a calendar of start and potential completion dates in between. All this forms part of planning the investigation.

A useful way of delineating what is to be done, by whom and when it needs to be done is to create a framework for the investigation. This will serve as a guide to the investigator and the employer while managing the investigation. The following table is designed as an illustrative example only:

ACTIVITIES TABLE		
Activity	Responsible Person	Timeframe
1.Request video footage from incident location	Security Manager	5 October 2016
2.Reserve a room for investigation interviews	Divisional Administrator	2 October 2016
3.Contact outside experts for forensic analysis	Investigations Manager	10 October 2016
4.Analyse applicable organisational policies	Human Resources Officer	15 October 2016
5.Compile a list of witnesses	Employee Relations Officer	12 October 2016
a.Make interview appointments	Investigations Manager	4 October 2016
b.Communicate with IT department to gather evidence	Investigations Manager	7 October 2016

NB: This framework makes it easy for the investigator to report on progress made to the accounting officer or any other structure where a report is to be delivered. This is in accordance with the terms of reference for the initiation, handling, and management of the investigation and ensures accountability to all parties. It also shows that the investigator can work with team members from IT, legal services and others, depending on the terms of reference, for the workplace investigation. In this example, an investigation team conducts the investigation.

Information collection[4]

When a complaint or report is received by the employer, alerting it to a possible violation of rules of conduct applicable in the workplace, a breach of organisational policy, national laws, or a collective agreement, it is important for this to be noted in the preliminary assessment of issues to be investigated. It is this analysis that will determine the scope of the investigation. In line with this, information collection during a workplace investigation will lead to the employer identifying:

- The sources of evidence to be presented, including documents.
- Witnesses who can be interviewed as part of the investigation.
- An employee handbook / organisational policy to be referenced.
- Industry good practice in investigating the incident, event, or occurrence.
- Whether or not there will be any need for expert input in the matter.

In respect of document management, it is critical that the investigator decides:

- Where documents will be stored.
- How these documents will be recorded.
- Which team members will have access to them.
- A chain of custody to protect the collected information (so that only specified people have access to specific documents).

All the above measures are important to ensure the integrity of the investigation. This comes into play in the event that a party claims that there has been tampering with the evidence by the employer organisation. As part of the chain of custody, the investigator must also determine who will have access to case information, who will have access to specified information, and who will not have access to information contained in the case file.

The investigator should also determine if law enforcement agencies, such as the SAPS, need to be involved straight away or at a later stage in the process. During the information collection stage it is possible to identify if a crime was committed or not. The timing of when to involve the SAPS and other law enforcement agencies is informed by whether there is a legal obligation to report a crime based on the regulations governing the conduct of business in a given sector or industry. This is more important for the private sector, if the business of the employer includes working with government, or if the misconduct, on the initial facts, might be seen to involve a threat to public safety.

Practice Guide

PRINCIPLES FOR CONDUCTING INVESTIGATION INTERVIEWS

1. During the introduction, inform employees you represent the employer.
2. Explain the general purpose and process of the investigation, as per the terms of reference.
3. Emphasise that the investigation is a fact-finding exercise.
4. Restate the importance of telling the truth and full disclosure.
5. Confirm that the employer is seeking the truth only.
6. Inform witnesses that no retaliation will be allowed by the employer.
7. Even though the investigation is confidential, management will be informed of the outcome, including law enforcement agencies if a crime is suspected.
8. Inform the witness that no foregone conclusions of guilt or innocence have been reached by the organisation, hence the investigation.
9. Advise the participant that the responsibility of a witness is to cooperate as required by law.
10. There is a directive to preserve documents as evidence and employer property.
11. The right to representation, or being accompanied, is allowed.
12. Start with open-ended questions to build rapport and ease into the interview.
13. Periodically summarise and review the story so far.

14. Concentrate on the facts of who, what, when, why, and where.
15. Use a chronological path.
16. Listen to the witness as they relate a story.
17. Consider getting written statements.
18. Prepare a summary of interview, after completion.

Interviewing the relevant parties[5]

This is part of the planning activities referred to in the table above:

- The investigator must first interview the person who made the complaint or reported the matter.
- If there are others named in the complainant's report, interview them as well.
- Following thereon, the investigator must interview the witnesses who claimed to have observed the incident. If additional witnesses are identified, interview them as well.
- Finally, the investigator must interview the subject of the investigation (a fellow employee, supervisor or manager).

The purpose of the interview is to find out the facts. This is done by identifying who did what that infringes on a policy or law, when the incident occurred, why things were done in a specific manner and where it happened. This inquiry is meant to facilitate the easy flow of the information, as well as to discover the sequential order of the story as narrated by the parties who are involved in the investigation.

An interview plan must therefore include information showing the name of the interview subject as well as the names of the witnesses, specified dates of events including details such as the time and place, where possible. More importantly, the investigator must be objective and refrain from inserting their personal views into the notes.

Furthermore, it is advisable that interviews be conducted at a neutral venue and in a private place. The interview room should be easily accessible to the subject of the interview and have little to no distractions, to enable complete concentration.

From a planning point of view, the investigator must prepare for the interview by ensuring that he follows a plan showing a list of witnesses to be interviewed, as well as when, where and by whom they will be interviewed. This plan must also include a list of questions the investigator will ask each one of the interviewees. All the prepared questions must reveal facts that:

- Relate the sequence of events in the witnesses' own personal words.
- Reveal the location of the incidents; including the date and time they occurred.
- Show the personal involvement of the witness as participant.
- Confirm or verify a story related by another person.
- Prove that all the questions addressed to one person were also addressed to another (consistency principle).

Making factual findings and recommendations

After the interviews have been conducted and the information collected, it is incumbent on the investigator to make findings of fact, based on the evidence adduced and information collected. A determination will have to be made showing whether there is a *prima facie* case to be answered by the subject of the investigation.

Alternatively, the investigator may come to the conclusion that the evidence is inconclusive and that the investigation cannot continue. This is all based on facts. These findings must help the employer to decide whether or not to take any action against the subject of the investigation. Conversely, it could also be used to motivate why the investigation should be closed if there are insufficient facts to substantiate the claims made against the subject.

The investigator can recommend some of the following courses of action to the employer:

- Institute disciplinary action where a *prima facie* case of misconduct exists.
- Suspend an employee as a precautionary measure (if allowed by the disciplinary code and procedure), based on an assessment of risks to the investigation.
- Suggest counselling or professional assessment of the employee.
- Refer the matter for mediation by an independent employment panellist, when colleagues are involved, as an intervention.
- Seek to involve the SAPS where it is suspected that a crime has been committed.
- Train employees, if that is a necessary intervention suggested by the investigator.

The above recommendations are to be included in a report, written and filed by the investigator, showing that interviews were conducted with witnesses, relevant documents were referenced and legal opinions sought to ensure compliance with investigation policy protocols.

The investigator must keep all the information collected during the investigation up to this point in a case file. This file should contain a comprehensive investigation report and interview notes that are legible and easy to read, but also demonstrates a logical progression of interviews and supporting documentation.

Investigation outcome letter to complainant

PRIVATE AND CONFIDENTIAL

Ms Portia Mukwevho

108 Swellendam Court

Jeff Masemola Street, Sunnyside

Pretoria, 0001

Dear Ms Mukwevho,

Outcome of Sexual Harassment Complaint Investigation

We are writing to let you know the outcome of our investigation.

We received your complaint on ________________ (Date) After meeting with you to talk about your concerns, we also met with your director ______________________ (name), and certain witnesses. We received all of the information and documents gathered in the investigation and have concluded that the complaint is SUBSTANTIATED / INCONCLUSIVE / UNSUBSTANTIATED [delete whichever is not applicable].

[Include if the complaint is substantiated]: As a result, we will be taking steps to make sure that the concerns you raised do not arise again in the future. For reasons of confidentiality, we cannot disclose all the steps we will be taking. But they include the following:

- List the steps that are not confidential. [Advise the respondent and the witnesses that the investigation is complete. Also mention that a report will be submitted to management along with fact findings and recommendations, as well as an executive summary.]

If you are not happy with the outcome of our investigation, you can ask that your complaint be reviewed by the Appeal Authority (MEC), using the appeal form in the disciplinary code and procedures for the public service, or refer the matter to the PSC thereafter.

If you have any pertinent questions or concerns about our investigation or its outcome, please let us know by contacting Mr. Joshua Lategan (Investigator) at ________________ (Telephone number)

Thank you for bringing your complaint to our attention.

Yours sincerely
Keith Jantjies (Lead Investigator)
Signature: ____________________________
Date: ________________________________

Post investigation activities[6]

It is a known fact that a workplace investigation is a process that includes many activities. This section of the chapter is an analysis of what needs to be done by the investigator and the employer to wrap up the process.

As part of the preparation done at the start of the investigation, a professional investigator must also allot time for communicating with the parties involved regarding what has been discovered in the course of the investigation. This should also give clarity on what was not discovered to be fact, as well as provide guidance in terms of the way forward for both the employer and the individuals concerned.

The resolution activities undertaken by the investigator include the following:

1. Informing the parties who participated that the investigation is complete.
2. Communicating the summary of the findings, as per the scope of the investigation.
3. Managing unhappy parties by informing them that they have recourse to the grievance procedure, should they wish to escalate matters internally or externally, to an alternative dispute resolution forum.
4. Thanking participants for their contribution to the investigation process.
5. Using the investigation process as a learning tool and an opportunity to review organisational culture in order to ensure that employees know their duties, management carry out their responsibilities, and all the parties are aware of their rights.

In summary

The organisational preparation must answer specific questions relating to the design, conceptualisation, and execution of the investigation. Who will investigate the matters under consideration? What issues will be investigated? What evidence needs to be collected to establish the facts and who will be interviewed as witnesses?

Model letter inviting an employee to an investigation meeting

Date: ____________________

Dear: ____________________

My name is ____________________ (Name of investigator) I am currently in the process of investigating allegations of:

- Sexual harassment raised against you by a subordinate.
- Breach of organisational policy on promotions.
- Improper conduct not befitting of a manager of (company name).

I am writing to invite you to attend an investigation meeting on (date of meeting), at (time of meeting), in (location of the meeting) so that I may discuss the matter with you.

In attendance at the meeting will be myself and (name of note taker), who will be present to take notes. Please bring with you any information that you think might be useful to the investigation.

If you wish, you may be accompanied by a trade union representative or a work colleague. However, your companion will not be able to answer questions on your behalf.

To ensure that the investigation can be conducted as fairly as possible we request that you help keep the matter and anything discussed at the investigation meeting confidential. Any breach of confidentiality may be a disciplinary offence.

If you are unable to attend the meeting please contact (name of investigator/ Manger / HR Department) as soon as possible, so that an alternative arrangement can be made.

Yours sincerely

Abraham Lincoln Mathe

Director: Ethics and Risk Management

Chapter 5

An Investigator's Preparation

Thoroughness. Terms of Reference compliance

"Being able to conduct an effective internal investigation is essential for the day to day operation of an organisation."

- Investigation Guide[1]

Introduction

There are different categories of workplace investigations that present employer organisations with challenges. These investigations mainly point to an alleged breach of the rules or policy of an organisation, or a violation of a collective agreement or law. When determining if there is a case of general misconduct to be answered, an investigator must be able to say with logical certainty that:

- The affected employee (the subject of the investigation) did not comply with a specific rule or standard, applicable in the workplace.
- This rule or standard was known to the employee as he attended information sessions pertaining to the employer's code of conduct,

where this was explained by the management of the organisation.

- Such rule or standard is reasonable, lawful, and not onerous.
- If the affected person was not aware of all the above, he is reasonably expected to have been aware that this type of behaviour is not acceptable in any workplace (e.g. theft, fighting on duty, etc.)
- The employer has previously charged other employees with misconduct when they were said to have committed similar acts. These acts are listed as acts of misconduct in the employee handbook, the disciplinary code, and/or the HR policy of the business.

The actual purpose of the investigation will be to 'get additional facts[2]' from the affected person, find out if there are any witnesses that can testify to the events in question, and check what the organisational policy provisions are in this instance. The next step will be to determine whether this matter can be handled by a single investigator, or if there is a need for an investigation team to be appointed by the employer.

TERMS OF REFERENCE DOCUMENT

1. Identify the matters to be investigated, keeping in mind the time limit on the investigation, as well as what falls outside the scope of the investigation.
2. Set out the nature of the allegations / issues to be investigated.
3. Indicate who the investigator will be.
4. State what process will be followed. If you will be using an independent investigator, state whether the employer is still responsible for the design, execution and roll out of the investigation.
5. Refer to the relevant work rules, codes, policies and procedures.
6. Where possible, identify who should be investigated (the list is flexible).
7. Supply timeframes, even though these are not cast in stone.
8. Clarify that the role of the investigator is not the same as that of the decision maker.
9. Make it clear that anyone can have a support person or union representative at the interview meeting, and at any other time during the process.
10. Advise who the draft report will be given to for comment, prior to its finalisation.
11. Advise who the sponsor (initiator) is, including the manager responsible for managing the process.
12. List the contact person who is responsible for administrative issues relating to the handling of the investigation.

Role of the investigator

The role of the investigator will be clarified as including a review of the relevant documents; identifying who should be interviewed; preparing interview questions for each witness; conducting the interviews, as per the investigation plan; and ensuring legal compliance with applicable laws as well as the investigation policy.

Review of relevant laws including employer policies and procedures

It has been said that a workplace investigation is the 'process in which an investigator gathers factual information based on allegations and provides a sound, factual basis for decisions by management'[3]. In this section of the chapter, we seek to unpack the basics of investigating unsatisfactory / poor work performance allegations brought against an employee by management.

To begin with, it will be useful for us to provide the reader with a definition of unsatisfactory work performance. In essence, this refers to a situation where an employer claims that the identified employee's productivity and contribution to organisational performance falls below the required standard.

It then becomes the responsibility of an investigator to find out the factual basis for such an allegation. Procedurally, this means that the one who alleges must prove. Therefore, the investigator will seek to find out whether or not the employee failed to meet a performance standard; and if the employee did not meet the performance standard, whether or not (i) the employee was aware, or could reasonably have been expected to be aware of the required performance standard; (ii) whether the employee was given a fair opportunity to meet the required performance standard. This is the first activity to be undertaken by the investigator, by way of interviews with the employer. If it is confirmed that the employer has complied with these procedural requirements, then a case of unsatisfactory work performance can be opened.

The required standards of performance would naturally be contained in an employee's performance agreement, a contract of employment as well as the employer / workplace annual plan, including the organisation's performance management policy guidelines[4]. All these documents represent a legal minefield that must be navigated by the investigator in order to make factual findings.

The next activity in this enquiry is for the investigator to seek to establish the cause of this poor work performance. This is done by continuous interviewing of the employer representative, as well as the affected employee, as required by the rules of natural justice, including the organisation's investigations protocol (where it exists).

When interviewing the affected employee, it is necessary for the investigator to ask him to give his side of the story in answer to the allegations made by the employer. This interview will be designed to check if the employer complied with its own performance management procedures, which requires mainly that:

- Management hold a meeting with the affected employee, in order to get 'immediate verbal feedback each time poor performance is observed[5]'.
- The employer has in place systems, processes and procedures to set performance targets to be achieved by the employee, periodically.
- The employer set performance goals, standards and deadlines for achievement of such, in order to seek proof of who is responsible for the poor work performance, between the affected person and the employer.

- Counselling, mentoring and training be given to the employee, focusing on strategies to improve work performance, if it is shown that there is unsatisfactory performance on the part of the employee.

In the event that the employer can show plainly that it complied with all these legal steps, then the investigator is within his rights to inform the employer by way of an interim report that there is a case of poor work performance to be answered. As such, the employer can bring charges against the employee, in line with the organisation's disciplinary code and procedures[6].

In a nutshell, the process to conduct a poor work performance investigation entails: undertaking a preliminary assessment of issues raised to determine whether a *prima facie* case exists or not; developing an investigation framework; gathering information to assist the employer to make an informed decision, as well as to apply the applicable standard of proof in employment matters, that is, the "balance of probabilities" principle.

Identification of the specific factual and legal questions to be resolved

Best practice is defined as 'particularly excellent or aspirational management policies, procedures and practices[7]' that are not minimal or necessarily legally mandated. It is necessary to demonstrate how to conduct a legally compliant workplace investigation by developing a step-by-step approach that can be used by the practitioner.

A part of that demonstration is tackling the issue of investigating financial misconduct in the workplace. This category of offences includes bribery, corruption, fraud and grand theft (misappropriation of assets)

– phenomena we are all faced with daily in South Africa. An employee found guilty of any of these offences faces the possibility of dismissal. To begin with, we recommend the use of a Six Point Investigation Process[8]. The objective is to show the practitioner how to get it right from the beginning, by way of telling an anecdotal story, as a case study.

Point 1: Initial Analysis

- Who is alleged to have committed an offence?
  The main character in this story is Ms Priya Subramani, a Chartered Accountant and Head of Private Banking employed by the Bank of Babylon in Cape Town.

- What is the alleged violation?
  The affected person is alleged to have committed misconduct referred to as 'misappropriation of assets'. This is what the investigator must list in the complaint form.

- Is it necessary to investigate?
  The disciplinary code and procedure of the employer classifies the alleged offence as gross misconduct, which means that there is a possibility of dismissal. Therefore, it is a requirement that the employer investigate, in accordance with Item 4(1) of the *Code of Good Practice: Dismissal* in Schedule 8 of the LRA, 66 of 1995 (as amended).

- Are there any internal / external considerations or reporting deadlines to be factored into the planning of the investigation?
  If the affected person is a member of SAICA, it means that she is subjected to their code of conduct and disciplinary processes too.

The banking sector is also regulated by the Financial Sector Conduct Authority (FSCA). This means that a crime has probably been committed, hence the need to report this matter to the SAPS as soon as practically possible.

- Is there a need for any immediate action?
  Given that the allegations are very serious, it is necessary to suspend the affected person on a precautionary basis, as provided for in the disciplinary code of the employer, in order to successfully investigate the matter as well as avoid a situation where Ms Subramani interferes with witnesses by intimidating her subordinates.

- What is the single point of accountability (SPA) to oversee the investigation?
  The CEO, Douglas Vermaak, is the accounting officer who must approve the drafted terms of reference. Additionally, the investigation will be led by the Investigations Manager, Mr. Mkhuseli Mankayi, who happens to be the Head of Employee Relations. They will be assisted by 2 employee relations practitioners and an internal ICT investigator. The Bank's attorney of record, Mr. Keith Jantjies, will be overseeing the investigation to ensure compliance with relevant laws. In this case, the investigation will be conducted by a team.
- Who are the potential decision makers?
  As per the governance protocol of the company, the board's ethics sub-committee and the CEO will take final decisions on this matter, based on an investigation report that will be presented to them by the investigation team after completion of the process.

- Are there any special considerations?
  The affected person is a member of the Financial Sector Union of South Africa (FISUSA) that must be informed of the planned

investigation, as a courtesy and as per the organisational rights agreement negotiated between the employer and the union. At this point the identity of the whistle-blower who alerted the company to this malfeasance will have to be kept secret as per the confidentiality and ethics policy of the organisation.

- What must be preserved immediately?
  All printouts of reports showing the transactions approved by the affected person, a list of accounts in the employee's portfolio and access to the employee's personal computer must be restricted to the investigation team only.

- Confidentiality protection?
  The decision to suspend the employee on a precautionary basis must be confidential. It must also be followed by a memo to her subordinates and colleagues internally, written by the accounting officer, explaining the rationale for the suspension.

In order to manage the investigation, it is advisable that a meeting be called between the CEO and the suspected employee, who will have to be suspended immediately. A typical meeting, like the one to suspend Ms Priya Subramani on a precautionary basis, will be handled with the use of a document like the one included here, as a guide for management.

Practice Guide

ADMINISTRATIVE SUSPENSION MEETING SCRIPT FOR MANAGEMENT

You have been asked to attend this meeting because I must advise you that you are suspended from duty, on a precautionary basis, with immediate effect. This has been decided based on the allegations that you may have:

- You allegedly misappropriate assets belonging to Mr. Roger Scott, a client of the Bank of Babylon, equivalent to the value of R3 million between April - JUNE 2014.

Please note that this suspension is on full pay and it should not be regarded as a disciplinary measure. The decision to administratively suspend you has been made in order to allow a full investigation to be undertaken promptly.

Under the terms of the suspension you must not enter any Bank of Babylon premises unless it is to do so as a service user, to visit a relative, meet with a trade union representative, if you are a member or for a scheduled meeting with the investigator.

You are advised to refrain from contacting any member of staff where this contact may be considered as influencing the investigation / disciplinary process. You will be able to contact your legal representative or shop steward for the duration of your suspension.

An investigation officer has been allocated to undertake a full and thorough investigation into this matter and you will be advised of who this is in a letter confirming the outcome of this meeting. The investigation will be carried out as speedily as possible and will be carried out in accordance with the Bank of Babylon Disciplinary Code and Procedure for Senior and Executive Management, a copy of which is here [*give individual a copy of the policy*]. Your suspension will likely not last more than (30) thirty days. If the administrative suspension needs to be extended beyond thirty days, you will be contacted and advised of the situation and thereafter kept informed of any further delay.

Whilst on precautionary suspension you will not be permitted to work for any other organisation during your substantive contracted hours of employment with the Bank of Babylon. You are also not permitted to work for any of the contractors servicing Bank of Babylon whilst on precautionary suspension.

During the period of the administrative suspension you must remain available for any necessary fact-finding interview(s) and for a disciplinary hearing, should that be appropriate. More importantly, you must keep the Bank of Babylon informed of any change of address.

Annual leave cannot usually be taken during the suspension period without prior authorisation from the Board Chairperson who will liaise with the investigator to determine whether your request for annual leave will be granted.

If you are medically unfit during your suspension you must report this to the Board Chairperson. You will be required to provide medical certificates to support your claim of sickness and these should be forwarded to the board chairperson. In addition, you may be referred to the employer's chosen medical practitioner to determine if you are sufficiently fit to proceed with the disciplinary hearing or not, should this be necessary.

Do you understand the terms of the administrative suspension? [Record any questions and responses. These are to be included in the outcome letter following the meeting.]

I must advise you that your IT account will be frozen whilst you are on precautionary suspension. I must also now take from you any Bank of Babylon property. I have a form which we must complete, taking note of the items you have returned. You will be sent a copy of this form.

You will receive confirmation of this meeting in writing, including your precautionary suspension letter within forty-eight (48) hours.

Do you have any questions about the process?

Please confirm your current address and telephone number to ensure that our records are up to date.

Do you need to collect any of your personal belongings? Are you able to drive?

You are then required to leave Bank of Babylon premises immediately.

CLOSE MEETING

Additionally, the subordinates must be reminded of their contractual obligations to preserve company interests. Hence the need to refrain from discussing the matter of alleged executive misconduct with anyone, except the investigators.

Point 2: Appointing an Investigator

The investigations policy or protocol will guide the organisation. It details the criteria to be used to appoint the investigation manager, who may be assisted by a team of professionals with the requisite skills; qualifications and competencies to enable them to discharge their duty of gathering facts.

It must be remembered that privilege arises when there is the involvement of an attorney, a client seeking legal advice, or the possibility of privileged communication between the parties in anticipation of litigation in a court of law, for or against the employer.

In this instance, where there is a possibility of involving law enforcement agencies to combat the identified financial misconduct from a criminal law viewpoint, it is necessary that the investigation manager work hand in glove with the attorney of record engaged by the employer, from the beginning.

To claim attorney-client privilege in a workplace investigation process, it is important that the lawyers' notes from the Investigation be classified as such, by designating them as advice to the client (the employer organisation).

Point 3: Planning the Investigation

The role of the investigations manager in this matter will be to:

- Thoroughly review the relevant policies and procedures of the employer as they apply to the matter(s) to be investigated as alleged misconduct.
- Identify who should be interviewed as potential witnesses.
- Prepare a list of interview questions to be posed to each witness.

- Conduct the interviews, as per the investigation plan outlined at Chapter 3.
- Keep legible and clearly written notes of the interview.
- Ensure that the alleged crime scene is secured[9] – misappropriation of assets is a crime – by ensuring that evidentiary materials and documents are kept safe.
- Mitigate all risks to the investigation, as part of the risk management plan, and ensure confidentiality.

As explained, planning an investigation is part of the science of achieving a successful workplace investigation. As such, the plan must show who will be informed of work in progress. This is part of the communications aspect of the plan.

As a fit-for-purpose plan, the workplace investigation process is designed to ensure that all the identified steps are included in the execution. For instance, the order of interviews should be arranged in such a way that it follows a predetermined format to ensure a logical development of the facts. This level of thoroughness will have to be shown in the case file emerging after the completion of the investigation.

Point 4: Fact Finding, Interviewing and Re-interviewing

By definition, a workplace investigation is a fact-finding exercise. The objective of its conceptualisation and design is to find out the truth about what happened when there are different versions of an alleged event. As such, the complainant interview answers will be linking the affected person to an allegation, such as the 'misappropriation of assets' in the case of Priya Subramani that we are presently analysing.

In order to determine factually and legally whether there is a *prima facie* case of financial misconduct to be answered, as defined in the employer disciplinary code and procedure, the investigator must confine himself to asking interview questions relating to the official duties of the affected employee. This line of questioning must focus on:

- The sequence of events, as explained by the employee.
- The location of the incidents, including the time period of its occurrence.
- The personal involvement of the employee by giving an A-Z picture of what happened, in order to differentiate perception from reality.
- An answer regarding whether there are any witnesses that can be linked to the matter at hand, to verify or dispute the story.
- Each witness giving a response by asking them the same questions.

Procedurally, all the interviews are to be conducted on neutral ground, in order to avoid allegations of intimidation by a witness who is affected by the complaints raised against them. It is advisable that the allegations be kept in a complaint form, in the case of allegations of misconduct.

The investigation of the allegations regarding misappropriation of assets must be informed by reference to the following organizational documents: the commercial crime law that is violated is the Prevention and Combatting of Financial Crimes Act; your contract of employment provision relating to Ethical Conduct at Work; the Bank of Babylon Policy on the Protection of Client Assets by Employees.

More importantly, if it happens that there is a gap between the information collected during the first investigation meeting, and what is required to make a determination of a *prima facie* case, it becomes necessary for the investigator to re-interview all the parties again, especially the complainant, the affected person, and witnesses.

The objective of the re-interview is to reassess the process of the investigation as per the overview in the investigation plan. The investigator must thereafter go through his notes to see what specifics have been left out, by comparing statements to documentary evidence and physical exhibits. It also means going back to key subjects in the interview and asking who else might be able to verify the statements made. The investigator will also have to review any employment relations governance documents at this point.

Point 5: Analysing the Evidence

The investigator must ensure that there is a factual basis for decision makers to arrive at a conclusion that there is a *prima facie* case of misconduct to be answered by Ms Subramani. This means identifying the policies of the employer that have been breached by this gross misconduct, listing the documents that have not been complied with, showing the reporting rules that have been violated, and showing potential charges that can be formulated.

The investigator must allow each piece of evidence collected, including witness statements and the complaint form to be analysed by the employer attorney to ensure that there is compliance with legal prescripts and rules relating to the interpretation of evidence. The purpose is to find out if there is a missing link between collated evidence or a conflict between what is said by witnesses and what happened.

The analysis of evidence must point to the findings of fact, with the investigation team double checking the quality of evidence received and asking if it can stand the test of time under cross-examination, at a disciplinary hearing, or at an external dispute resolution forum such as the CCMA or the Labour Court.

Point 6: Reporting

The next activity after analysing evidence is for the investigator and his assistants to draft a report to the board of directors and the CEO, informing them that the process has reached a stage where they can objectively give a picture of what happened. Such a report must talk directly to the agreed terms of reference, as received from the accounting officer, Mr. Vermaak.

The investigation report must be crafted based on a standard checklist, as per the investigation plan submitted by the investigator and approved by the organisation's leadership. Among other important issues, it must state the case information collected, refer to the case notes of the compiler, and contain interview summaries and exhibits to support findings, as well as recommendations.

Before submitting a report to the decision makers it is necessary that the author develop a structure for the report, so that it can clearly be demonstrated what could be proven factually and what could not be proven, in relation to the allegations. Importantly, the report must include an executive summary, terms of reference, the allegations as per the complaint form, as well as the findings of fact.

Read more about this component of the workplace investigation process in Chapter 9.

Practice Guide

INVESTIGATION REPORT

This is a template investigation report that an investigator may adapt to suit the circumstances of the investigation.

Introduction	Investigation authorised by: Name and Designation __________________________ __________________________ Investigator: Name and Designation __________________________ __________________________ Date investigation started: __________________________ Terms of reference: Attach as addendum, especially if they were amended. Background to the investigation: Brief overview of the matter __________________________ __________________________ __________________________ __________________________

Process of investigation	The investigation process: Explain how the investigation was authorised ____________________________ ____________________________ Evidence collected: ____________________________ Evidence not collected: Including the reason why it was not collected ____________________________ Persons interviewed: (List all names) ____________________________ ____________________________ Persons not interviewed: (Witnesses that could not be interviewed and why) ____________________________ ____________________________ Anonymised statements: (If any, explain why and provide details of any enquiries into witness) ____________________________ ____________________________

INVESTIGATION FINDINGS	Summary of written and physical evidence: (Name and summarise each document contained, set out how the evidence supported or did not support your findings and why) ________________________ ________________________ Summary of witness evidence: (Name and summarise each witness statement, quote from statement where relevant, set out how the witness statement supported or did not support your findings and why) ________________________ ________________________ Facts established: (Detail what the investigation has established) ________________________ ________________________ Facts that could not be established: Detail any part of the investigation that was inconclusive ________________________ ________________________

	Mitigation factors: Detail if there were any mitigation factors uncovered that are relevant to the investigation ______________________ ______________________ Other relevant information: Detail any other information that is relevant to the matter ______________________ ______________________
CONCLUSION (if required)	Recommendations: Formal Action / Informal Action / No action required .... Further details on recommendations: (Such as the type of action suggested. For example, a formal disciplinary meeting, or any other recommendations related to the matter. In disciplinary matters, the investigation should not recommend a possible sanction. This should only be considered in a disciplinary hearing.) ______________________ Investigator's Signature: __________ Date: ______________

Supporting documents	List of all documents collected as part of the investigation and included in the report: ____________________ ____________________

Careful selection of an investigation team

When an investigation deals with financial misconduct at work where it is alleged that there has been asset misappropriation, as in the example of Priya Subramani, it is important that the organisation pays close attention to the terms of reference. It serves as a roadmap of what must be factually proven by the employer.

A multidisciplinary investigation team appointed by the employer will have to include members with managerial skills (knowledge of standard operating procedures at the bank), technical competencies (ICT specialisation), as well as malfeasance investigation skills (a professional trained in the application of labour law provisions), among others[10]. The members who possess the above mentioned skills will constitute the core of the investigation team.

The team will have to be led by a qualified fraud examiner who is an experienced financial economics professional, but also trained in the applicable banking laws and regulations. Finally, the investigation team must include a commercial law attorney drawn from internal counsel. The attorney must be able to advise the organisation on how to approach the civil courts to recover the losses of the bank, and how to institute a criminal prosecution against the accused employee if it is established that a crime may have been committed.

It will further be required that the investigation team to be competent in handling information classified as attorney-client privileged, so that it remains classified. This is where the participation and advice of a professional lawyer becomes relevant to the investigation process. The same attorney determines the information included in the final report to be presented to the leadership of the organisation, as well as what the investigation file must contain. Bear in mind the possibility that the team may have to share some of the information collected by the investigation with the legal representatives of the accused employee in a court of law.

This investigation team would not be complete without the inclusion of an administrator to assist the team with the control and logging of collected data as part of an information management activity. All the documents produced by the investigation constitute evidence to be used for reporting the outcome and preparing for litigation, should that become necessary at a later stage either during or after the investigation process has been completed.

SECURING INVESTIGATION FILES AND RECORDS

Maintain a separate investigation file containing:

1. All interview notes
2. All communications with witnesses
3. All written witness statements
4. All documents that support / refute the allegations
5. The investigation report
6. Any recorded statements and transcripts
7. Relevant organisational policies
8. Applicable laws and collective agreements
9. Letters to affected person (accused)
10. Letter of appointment as investigator
11. Investigation terms of reference
12. Letters to the complainant

Box 4

Establishment of a preliminary logical order and timeline for interviews

This activity is part of the plan of the investigator. Using the matter of alleged asset misappropriation, included as a case study here, the logical order of interviews will be demonstrated as follows:

Interview 1:

This will be a fact gathering exercise involving a discussion with the whistleblower that raised the Bank's awareness regarding a suspected case of embezzlement. It will be undertaken confidentially by the lead investigator.

Interview 2:

This is a meeting between the investigator and the alleged victim of the fraud perpetrated by the affected employee (Priya Subramani), to find out what happened, as provided for in the terms of reference drafted by the employer.

Interview 3:

A workplace interview meeting between Priya Subramani and the lead investigator, to seek an explanation for the allegations made against her by both the victim and the whistleblower.

Interview 4:

A meeting between the investigator and the head of security for the Bank of Babylon, to seek information about standard operating procedures relating to employee access to client accounts.

Interview 5:

A meeting between the investigator and the supervisor of the affected employee to gather information about the reporting structure of the private banking division, as well as any systems relating to the allocation of tasks as per this structure.

Interview 6:

The last interviews will be coordinated by the investigator to seek clarity on how private banking transactions are managed. This will include meetings with colleagues of Priya Subramani, as well as from the ICT department, about the procedures followed in managing client accounts electronically.

Determining the Credibility of a Witness

PLAUSIBILITY

Is the witness's version of the facts believable?

DEMEANOUR

Does the witness seem to be telling the truth?

MOTIVE

Does the person have a reason to lie?

CORROBORATION

Are there documents or other witnesses that support the witness's version of events?

PAST RECORD

Does the alleged wrongdoer have a past record of inappropriate conduct?

Box 5

All of the above interviews should be conducted at the head office of the Bank of Babylon, away from the actual workplace where the alleged incidents took place.

Each one of the listed persons should be interviewed individually. The subject of the interview will have to be informed of the nature of the allegations; the investigator's role during the investigation; how confidentiality will be maintained; and the terms of reference for the investigation, including how the process will be 'managed after the interviews[11]'. At the same time the interviewed employees should be informed of their rights as employees.

As part of the plan, the investigator should also ensure that the interviews are completed within 21 working days – the period prescribed in the investigation protocol of the organisation. Where the investigation is incomplete, this period can be extended to no more than thirty working days.

Preparation of a tentative list of questions and matters to cover in interviews[12]

It has been noted previously that a workplace investigation will not be considered legally compliant if the employer is unable to show that interviews were conducted with all the key parties. It must be clear that all parties involved had a role in uncovering the facts about the issues being investigated. These parties include the complainant who brought the matter to the attention of the employer, as alleged in the complaint form; the affected person who is being accused of wrongdoing; as well as witnesses who are in possession of relevant information or claim to have witnessed the incident.

If we are to return to the case referred to earlier, where it is alleged that Ms Priya Subramani committed an offense related to asset misappropriation, it will be critical that the investigation team prepare a list of questions to be posed to each one of the identified role players involved in the case. The intended purpose is to:

- Determine if there is any truth to the claim of financial malfeasance.
- Establish the total amount of assets allegedly embezzled, including the modus operandi of the alleged perpetrator.
- Facilitate the removal of the wrongdoer from the premises of the employer, given the fact that the allegation relates to gross misconduct,

as classified in the employer disciplinary code and procedure.

- Seek to recover the misappropriated assets through the early involvement of the state's law enforcement agencies, who can apply for the freezing of assets that have been acquired as proceeds of crime.
- Get to the bottom of what happened, with the ultimate aim of taking any necessary administrative action to protect the employer's interests during the investigation.

The list of questions to be drafted will have to consistently cover themes relating to the background of each person – especially what their terms and conditions of employment are at the workplace. This will be done after the introductions are dealt with and the purpose and scope of the process have been explained to the interviewees.

- When interviewing the accused person, it is advisable that the investigator cover the following areas of interest:
- The extent of the malfeasance. Zoom in on what happened on a specific date as well as the amounts involved, to determine when exactly the accused started with the embezzlement scheme.
- Find out the motive for the asset misappropriation. Ask the accused to explain why he committed the alleged offence, considering the fraud triangle theory developed by Donald Cressey. (Other people's money (montclair: patterson smith, 1973)
- Determine if the accused was working alone or whether he had any accomplices, either at work or externally.
- Ask questions that will unravel the modus operandi. Find out the methods used to accomplish such a complex operation, in order to prevent a recurrence in future.
- Encourage the cooperation of the accused by pointing out during the

course of the interview that your preliminary investigation uncovered specific facts and information about what is being investigated.

- Formulate questions in such a way as to show that the employer has physical information to back the claim of embezzlement and ask for an explanation of specific incidents and events.
- Utilize open-ended questions that draw out information.

PRELIMINARY INVESTIGATION PLAN

Investigator	Mkhuseli Mankayi
Terms of reference	Investigate allegations of asset misappropriation levelled against Ms Priya Subramani. Determine what happened when Mr Roger Scott lost investments and savings equivalent to R3 million between April – June 2014. Make recommendations on factual and legal issues. Advise Bank of Babylon about what can be done differently to avoid a recurrence of such misconduct (SOP and organisational culture).
Provisional timetable	11 July – 11 August 2014
Policies and procedure to review and follow	Banking & Investment Policy; Ethics & Business Conduct Guidelines; Employee Handbook; telephone calls.
Issues that need to be explored / clarified	Whether any other person(s) were involved; motivation for the financial malfeasance.

Sources of evidence to be collected	Computer records where Ms Subramani's password was used during the period under review; video footage of the Bank from the period under review, etc.
Persons to be interviewed (including planned order of interviews)	Head of private banking at head office. Supervisor of private banking at Cape Town branch. Head of security at the Bank. Supervisor of Ms Subramani at the Cape Town branch.
Investigation meetings further arrangement (when / where / notes to be taken)	12 July, 15 July, 18 July, 20 July, 02 August, 06 August, 12 August, and 16 August.
Persons to supply own statements	Supervisor, Mrs Boniswa Maphalala.
Investigation meetings to be completed by	22 August 2014
Reporting	Initial report to be complete and submitted by 30 August 2014.
Communications	Outcome letters to be sent to all the parties on 30 August 2014, asking them to make factual comments on the initial report by no later than 7 September 2014. If they fail to do so, a final report will be prepared and used as basis for decisions by the organisation. All this is to be done on a 'need to know basis'.

In summary

This chapter is about what the investigation manager will be doing to implement the mandate received from the organisation. Such a mandate is defined in the terms of reference agreed to between the employer and the investigator.

The scope and purpose of the investigation will guide the investigator on how to start with the process, suggest the time period during which to carry out the investigation, as well as the methodology to use in order to get to the facts.

The investigator is therefore expected to set up an information management system detailing how the received information and evidence is to be safeguarded and recorded for retrieval at a later stage. This system should show which files will be kept by the investigator as custodian of the process. In this regard, it is advisable that all files are kept separate from the final report to be submitted to the organisation, and summary copies to be handed over to the parties involved in the investigation. All this planning information is to be kept in a preliminary investigation plan that can be updated as the investigation progresses.

Finally, as part of the investigation risk management processes the employer, based on advice from the investigation manager, must decide if there is a need for the precautionary suspension or transfer of any of the parties involved in the investigation. The preliminary investigation plan must also show how communications between the organisation and the investigator, as well as the parties involved, are to be managed throughout the process.

Chapter 6

Handling an Investigation Meeting

Objectivity. Managing Witnesses

"An investigation interview is a conversation designed to gather information and evidence that is accurate, relevant and complete from: subjects / suspects, victims, complainants, informants, witnesses."

- I-Sight
Investigation Interview Techniques

Introduction

It is fundamentally important that the investigation meeting be handled with tact. The approach to be used by the investigator involves doing the following:

1. Introducing the investigator as an employer representative, by saying something like this: "I am investigating an allegation of sexual harassment within the SCM Directorate. I would like to ask you and some of your colleagues a few questions about it". The objective of this approach is to lay out the reason for the meeting without giving away information already in possession of the employer.

This is especially applicable when meeting with the subject of the investigation.

2. In principle, it is necessary to say upfront that the interview is conducted to get full and honest answers in order to get to the bottom of the allegations made.
3. The next step is for the investigator to explain the issues being investigated. This is done by specifically mentioning the points, as stipulated in the terms of reference, and in reference to the allegations made in the complaint form. It is essential for the investigator to be objective. It must be clearly explained that the investigation meeting serves as an opportunity for all parties to state their side of the story.
4. When interviewing the complainant the investigator must still seek to find out what happened; where the incident that is alleged occurred (location); ask for the date when this occurred (on or about); request an explanation of how the allegation played itself out in their own words; and whether there is any explanation for why this occurred. This is so the investigator can better understand the issues the complainant objects to.
5. When talking to witnesses the investigator must consistently apply the same principle of seeking just the facts. He must assist them in sharing the information they may have about the sexual harassment claim.

Witnesses must be asked to explain if they were physically at the same place where the incident happened, or whether they heard about it via other people.

In addition, it is essential that the investigator allow the accused person to be accompanied by a shop steward or a work colleague, especially in unionised workplaces. This is to ensure that the employer is protected against accusations of 'interfering with the right to representation[1]', as part of the *audi alterem partem* principle in investigations.

As part of conducting this workplace investigation, the investigator needs to fully understand the role of the workplace representative, which includes the following responsibilities:

- Supporting the employee before, during and after the interview by clarifying the procedure, reassuring the person of his rights, and providing information such as a code of conduct or policy.
- Ensuring due process is followed throughout the interview, that the person is not asked irrelevant questions, and that he is not ensnared or miss-led by the investigator.

It is important that the investigator knows what to do when the representative tries to overstep his role. This often happens when the representative attempts to answer questions on behalf of the member, or attempts to put the investigator on the back foot by testing his understanding of the disciplinary code and procedure of the employer. The response to the above is for the investigator to:

- Emphasise that all the questions asked by the investigator are required to be answered by the affected employee alone.
- Address the questions directly to the accused person by facing them, without being disrespectful to the representative.
- Note the behaviour of the representative, in writing, with the intention of reporting on it when the interview is complete and analysed.
- Inform the employee that the interview will continue irrespective of the behaviour of the representative (with their permission of course).
- Remind the representative of each person's role in the interview and ask that each party abide by their role.
- Adjourn the meeting and talk privately with the representative if problems persist. This should be done in order to find common ground, in accordance with protocol as per the investigation policy of the employer.

Practice Guide

GUIDING PRINCIPLES FOR CONDUCTING WORKPLACE INVESTIGATIONS

1. Absence of conflict of interest. It can be actual, perceived or potential. A decision maker, who has a conflict of interest, whether real or perceived, should remove himself from the decision-making process and a new decision maker must then be appointed.
2. Clarity, ethics and transparency. Ensuring that parties to an investigation are always treated fairly and with respect.
3. Procedural fairness / natural justice, comprising the following three principles:
   a. The right to be heard. A person must be given enough information to know the case against him and be given the opportunity to present his case.
   b. The right to an unbiased decision maker.
   c. The right to have a decision based on evidence and with reasons for the decision.

   Procedural fairness requires that a fair and proper procedure be applied when a decision is made. It is necessary for the findings to be organisationally defensible and legally sound.
4. Confidentiality. Steps must be taken to safeguard the confidentiality of the investigation in the interest of the persons involved, and for the integrity of the investigation process.
5. Lawful. Ensuring provisions, directives, guidelines, policies, and procedures required by law are observed throughout the process.
6. Timely and proportionate. Investigations should conclude as

quickly as possible and endeavour to meet the benchmarks for timeliness.

7. Logical and justifiable. Findings and recommendations are supported by evidence. Reports are logical and provide a sound basis for decisions to be made on the merits of the case and on the balance of probabilities.
8. Separation of the roles of investigator and decision maker. The decision maker must come to an independent conclusion, based on the evidence presented by the investigator. It is the role of the investigator to present evidence in relation to the allegations. It is not the role of the investigator to make conclusions about:
   a. Whether there has been a breach of policy or legislation.
   b. Whether grounds for disciplinary action exist.
   c. What the appropriate next steps may be after the investigation.
9. Regular and transparent communication, including by:
   - Outlining the proposed process, estimated timeframes and obligations
   - Providing regular updates throughout the process
   - Keeping a record of any communication on file to demonstrate key parties who must be kept informed about the process
   - Applying the duty of care for all involved persons.

Adapted from Managing Workplace Investigations. A practical guide for the Queensland Public Sector. September 2018.

Explain the ground rules

It has been noted throughout this book that investigating is a step-by-step process. The starting point in the investigation meeting is an introduction which explains the terms of reference and background to the investigation. Hence, the importance of the investigator Letter of Appointment. At this stage the investigator does not need to reveal unnecessary details about the investigation, except that it is a 'fact-finding[2]' exercise.

Furthermore, the investigator must explain to the witness / employee that he is required to cooperate with the investigation, in line with the standard duties of the employee. Thus, it is advisable that the employee give full and honest answers to questions posed. This does not mean that the investigator, as an agent of the employer, must be aggressive in order to get the facts relating to the issues under investigation. It just means being persistent in asking for answers.

Abide by Terms of reference

The investigation meeting should be managed in terms of this document which shows the 'scope and purpose[3]' of the process. It legitimises the investigation as a legal undertaking driven by the organisation. The purpose is to build rapport between the witness and the investigator, thus seeking to get their cooperation without using more aggressive tactics.

Ensure Confidentiality

At the start of the investigation meeting it is critical that the investigator inform the participants that the investigation policy of the employer requires the discussions to be kept confidential. Hence, it is advisable that the witnesses do not discuss any issue arising out of the investigation with anyone other than their legal representative. In this way the integrity of the investigation will be protected, as well as the identity of the witnesses. However, there is no requirement to guarantee the employee of 'absolute confidentiality[4]', as the investigator is still required to report to the employer about work in progress.

Interview witnesses[5]

The employer is required to conduct interviews. A record of these interviews will be included in the final investigation report, showing who and what was discussed with the witnesses during interviews. All these interviews will have to be documented to prove their legitimacy.

This activity is critical in ensuring that the employer can demonstrate that it complied with the requirements of procedural fairness during the investigation. A key driver of proving such compliance is the notes made by the investigator throughout the process. These illustrate who was called into an investigation meeting, on what date, as well as the questions that were posed to the individual interviewee. A suggested template for interviewing witnesses could resemble this:

INVESTIGATION QUESTIONNAIRE TEMPLATE

1. What is the allegation?

____

____

2. What is the organisational policy regarding these types of allegations?

____

____

3. Who is the complainant(s)?

____

____

4. What position does he hold?

____

____

5. Who is the affected person (accused)?

____

____

6. What position does he hold?

____

____

7. Who should be interviewed? (Include the order of the interviews.)

____

____

8. Where should the interviews take place?

9. Are there any supervisors or managers I need to inform?

10. What possible issues may arise during the interview process?

11. Does anyone need to be suspended in order to stop unlawful behaviour?
Motivate the answer.

12. Do I need to freeze computer records? Motivate the answer.

13. Do I need to talk to the IT or Security Department?

14. What documents do I need to review?

Adapted from *I-Sight. 8 Internal Investigation Tips*, article by Joe Gerard.

A. Questions for complainant

In a case dealing with allegations of 'abuse of authority' by an executive manager, it is important for the investigator to advance strictly 'by the book', due to the risks involved and the potential impact on the employer organisation.

Procedurally, this means that the investigator should have issued written notices inviting the complainant to a formal investigation meeting, after having received a written complaint and undertaken a preliminary assessment of the issues mentioned in it.

At the first interview meeting, after the introductions, the investigator must inform the interviewee about the scope and purpose of the investigation as required by the organisational policy.

Secondly, the investigator must inform the complainant that the investigation is to be conducted in accordance with the terms of reference developed by the employer. These include investigating allegations of abuse of authority by the GM of Corporate Services, as alleged by the main complainant and two other employees in a complaint form received by the organisation on 2 June 2017. The purpose of this is to confirm, for the record, that the complainant accepts the terms of reference before the commencement of the interview.

Thirdly, it is necessary that the investigator confirm the organisational policy of non-retaliation in matters of this nature against any one of the parties. Also, to inform the complainant that the investigation is confidential but a report will be presented to the head of the department after the completion of the investigation. The complainant has a duty to cooperate as an employee.

Fourthly, the investigator should advise the complainant that he has the right to make a written statement, if that is his wish, confirming what he will be telling the investigator during the interview.

Fifth, it is advisable that the investigator confirm the background information provided during the forwarding of the complaint in writing, as well as the contact details provided. Therefore, some of the key questions to be asked of the complainant should include the following:

1. Whether the incidents complained about affected employment relations at the workplace in any way.
2. Whether the events related in the complaint form were witnessed by anyone. If the answer is yes; is it possible to share the contact details of such witnesses?
3. Is this the first time that these events have happened, or is it a recurrence? A follow up question will be to ask how many times this type of behaviour occurred previously, including locations of incidents.
4. It is important that the investigator ask if the complaint is documented anywhere. E.g., is there a hardcopy to access; electronic mail; phone texts; social media accounts; photographs, etc., to refer to?
5. Is the complainant aware of any other person who has been subjected to the same treatment of favouritism, besides the ones mentioned on the complaint form?
6. Are there any other issues, besides the official complaint, that the employee would like to be addressed during this investigation?
7. Furthermore, is there any additional information that the complainant would like the investigator to consider as part of the facts?
8. If the answer to the above question is negative, the investigator can ask the complainant if there is anything that he thinks can be added to the investigation, before closing the interview.

Given the fact that the interview of the complainant is part of a formal investigation process, the investigator must inform him of the way forward:

- There are other additional witnesses to be interviewed, which means that the investigation is still confidential until the matters are resolved.
- The proceedings are therefore not to be discussed with colleagues, outsiders, or family members, in order to protect the integrity of the investigation.
- Even though the interview is complete for now, if the complainant remembers anything, he is free to contact the investigator at the contact details included in the letter inviting him to the interview.
- Thank him for making time to attend the interview and close the meeting formally. Inform the complainant that the plan is for the investigation process to be finalised within the time period stipulated in the terms of reference letter discussed at the beginning of the interview.

INVESTIGATION FACT COLLECTION SHEET
(For managers and supervisors use only)

Instruction: This form is designed to be used by the investigator for preliminary data collection.

1. Complainant: ______________________ [Name]
Job Title: ________________________
Staff Number: ____________________
Business Unit / Directorate: ____________________
Location: ________________________________
Contact Tel.: _________________

2. Supervisor: ______________________ [Name]
Job Title: _______________________
Contact Tel.: ____________________

3. Representative: ___________________ [Name]
Designation: _________________
Contact Tel.: _________________

Who is involved?
Witnesses: ____________________________________
____

Management: __________________________________
____

Employees: ___________________________________
____

When did the issue(s) arise? (Dates and time)
____
____

Where did the incident(s) occur? (Location)

____

____

What happened? (Facts / background information / viewpoints)

____

____

Why is this allegedly a grievance / act of misconduct / poor work performance?
Is it a breach of one of the following?

Past practice relating to.____________________

____

Contract of employment ______________________

____

Law____

____

Collective agreement

____

____

How to remedy the situation: Is there a specific or general remedy demanded by complainant?

____

____

B. Questions for witnesses

Concerning the investigation into allegations of 'abuse of authority in hiring decisions', three key witnesses are also the complainants.
It is a procedural requirement that the investigator must start each interview with an individual witness on a separate sheet of notepaper, for filing and record keeping purposes[6]. It is also important that the investigator attempt to make eye contact often throughout the interview in order to show the interviewee that it is a conversation and not an interrogation.

Secondly, it is a requirement that the workplace investigator ask questions thematically. This is done by focusing on key points instead of a list of written questions that are pre-determined, but serve no purpose in getting to the facts.

Thirdly, it is also advisable that no more than one person is interviewed at a time, as the investigator is still required to take legible notes that will later be included in the case file.

When designing an interview for the witnesses, it is important for the investigator to include different types of questions, similar to these:

- Introductory questions that seek to establish rapport[7];
- Informational questions that are simply fact gathering[8];
- Assessment questions designed to solicit honest responses[9];
- Admission-seeking questions to establish witness credibility[10]; and,
- Closing questions that reconfirm facts[11].

C. Questions for the subject of the investigation[12]

The purpose of any workplace investigation is to seek just the facts about who was involved, what happened, where events occurred, and to uncover any other relevant information.

In this example of an allegation of 'abuse of executive authority', the following are some of the key questions to be asked of the subject of the investigation:

1. You are alleged to have committed an act of improper behaviour by appointing persons who are not qualified. Can you give me your version of the events?
2. Did anyone witness the events in question, as specified in the complaint?
3. What exactly did you say and do on the specified dates?
4. If you deny the allegations, can you offer any reason as to why the complainants would claim that you did what is alleged?
5. Are you aware of the company policy on recruitment?
6. Are there any witnesses that you would like me to interview?
7. Do you have any further relevant information that I can take into account during the investigation?
8. Are there any supporting documents that you have that can confirm what you told me about the events in question?

In summary

The framework for interviewing the key parties to the investigation is the torch that guides the investigator on how to handle an investigation meeting. (It is included here as Appendix 9.) This framework is designed in such a way that it shows the purpose for interviewing the complainant, the objective for talking with the witnesses, as well as the organisational plan for engaging the affected employee.

The objective of the investigation meeting is to find out the sequence of events as they led up to the trigger of the workplace investigation; to list the facts. To illustrate this, the investigator introduces the scope and purpose of the investigation to each interviewee. He then lists the issues to be investigated as per the complaint or grievance form.

Next an explanation of the trigger that led to the investigation is sought, using the five journalistic questions of who, what, where, when, and why. This is asked of all the interviewees in order to get a direct account of the events for the record. There has to be notes from the interviews, showing what was said, in context, by each of the parties who participated. The investigator also asks if the interviewee has any witnesses to corroborate his side of the story or any documentary proof he can present as evidence.

Finally, after the interview is completed the investigator is required to explain the employer's processes, information relating to the finalisation of the investigation, and related communication about the way forward. For the last time, all the participants should be reminded that the investigation is still confidential. Any breach of such confidentiality would be to invite disciplinary action, which may include dismissal from employment as per the investigation protocol.

GRIEVANCE INVESTIGATION NOTICE

[Date]
[Recipient's Name]
[Recipient's Address]

Dear [ ]

GRIEVANCE LODGED

I confirm that on: ________________ [Date] the organisation received your lodged grievance, dated: ________________ [Day, month, year], wherein you complained about: [state issue and refer to actual grievance form, letter, affidavit].

In accordance with the grievance rules of the public service, the employer will arrange a formal grievance meeting with you as part of the investigation into the issues you complained about.

In the meantime ________________ [Name of individual / line manager] has been appointed to investigate your grievance. Should you have any queries before you are invited to the formal grievance hearing, please contact him/her by telephone or email at: ____________________________ [Tel. no / e-mail address.]

As part of this investigation ________________ [Name of individual / line manager] may be required to interview potential witnesses and review documents. Please be assured that this matter will be kept confidential as far as possible and every witness will be instructed not to discuss this matter. However, as part of the investigation process, it will be necessary to inform witnesses that a grievance has been lodged.

Lastly, the organisation wishes to point out that no decision will be taken regarding your grievance until the investigation has been completed and you have had an opportunity to discuss your complaints formally at a grievance meeting.

Please note that you will be expected to attend work as normal while the investigation is continuing.

Yours sincerely
Mr. Peter Ramarutsi Raboroko
Signature: ______________________________
Chief Executive Officer
Asambe National Carriers
Date:______________________________

Section C

Home of Best Practice

Chapter 7

Gathering Evidence[1]

Law of Evidence

"Few managers are experienced at investigating workplace complaints. Others have insufficient time to handle complex, emotional cases on top of their existing workload. In addition, if the investigation is run by an employee of the organisation, there is a risk of perceived bias towards either the complainant or the accused employee."

- Workplace Investigations, Worklogic.

Introduction

By now it has become abundantly clear that conducting a workplace investigation is a mammoth task. It can be compared to entering a minefield with the objective of removing the landmines before they detonate and cause legal, reputational and financial risks to the employer. A lack of skills on the part of those responsible for the management of the employment relationship could make this task even more complicated than is necessary. Yet, it is a task that can be achieved so long as practitioners know what is to be done. This means answering the five questions of who, what, where, when, and why.

It is the answers to these same questions that give an investigator the required evidence to determine whether there is a *prima facie* case of misconduct to be answered or not. He will use this information to decide whether the matter should be laid to rest due to a lack of evidence, or reach the conclusion that the allegations were false, frivolous and vexatious. Only the evidence will show the way forward for the employer.

A sexual harassment case study[2]

Miss Zubeida Alamein, the receptionist at Asambe National Carriers who alleges that she is being sexually harassed by Gideon Dickson the Manager: Supply Chain Management. Given the fact that sexual harassment is regarded as gross misconduct in South Africa, it carries the ultimate penalty of dismissal. It is therefore important that the employer investigate the allegation formally as per the provisions of the *Code of Good Practice: Dismissal.* Part of the planning involved in this investigation will be for the employer to analyse potential risks to the process; such as, whether there is any possibility of retaliation by the alleged perpetrator, given his seniority. In addition, the employer investigation will have to identify the parties involved; list the sources of evidence available, as well as compile a table of activities to be undertaken in order to gather evidence.

WORKPLACE HARASSMENT INVESTIGATION INTERVIEW QUESTIONS

For complainant

Background Questions

- How long have you worked for Asambe National Carriers?
- What are some of the responsibilities of your role within the company?
- Was there a particular reason for you to take this position?
- How would you describe the workplace culture? Is it supportive?

Standard Incident Related Questions

- Who committed the alleged harassment?
- What exactly occurred, or was said?
- When did the incident occur?
- Is it still going on?
- Where did the incident occur?
- Why did the incident occur?
- Are there indicators that suggest a source motivation for the subject?
- How often did it occur?
- How did it affect you?
- How did you react?
- Has your job been affected in any way?
- Has anyone been treating you differently?
- Does anyone else have relevant information regarding this incident?
- Was there anyone present when the alleged harassment occurred?
- Did you tell anyone about it?

- Are you aware of any harassment complaints previously made against this person?
- Are there any notes, physical evidence, or other documentation regarding the incident(s) that you could provide us with?
- Is there any additional information pertaining to the incident you would like to discuss?

Adapted from, EEOC (Equal Employment Opportunities Commission, USA).

Applying the provisions of Item 4 (1) of the Code of Good Practice: Dismissal[3]

In respect of the case study referred to above, the investigator will have to enquire whether the affected person:

1. Contravened a rule or standard regulating conduct at Asambe National Carriers (the employer) or not?
    - The first port of call is to peruse the disciplinary code and procedure which lists acts of misconduct, in order to determine whether sexual harassment in the workplace is listed as prohibited behaviour.
    - The next inquiry will be to check if there is any organisational policy regulating sexual relations between colleagues, such as a Code of Conduct or a general harassment policy adopted by the employer.
2. Inquire as to whether the employer may dismiss an employee for the alleged offence

- In order to arrive at a determination, the investigator must find out what category misdemeanour the offence is as per the employee handbook.
- Is the allegation categorised as minor, a serious or gross misconduct (which carries the outcome of dismissal).
- As soon as the investigator has made a determination he must invite the affected person to an investigation meeting. This is done in order to ask for an explanation or a version of events that can show what happened between the affected person and the complainant.
- Only interviews using the right to be heard principle will reveal the truth.

3. The investigation does not have to be a formal sitting
   - The affected person, the complainant and their identified witnesses can be asked to make written statements or invited to a workplace investigation meeting. At this meeting they will be asked, individually, to relate the events that led to the investigation (based on organisational policy).
4. Procedurally, the investigator must notify the parties of an investigation.
   - The first requirement is for the complainant to record the complaint in writing.
   - The affected person will then be informed about the matter in writing.
   - The investigator will also inform the employee that he may bring a representative or a support person to the investigation meeting.
   - It is these discussions that will form the backbone of the evidence gathered.

NOTICE TO ATTEND A GRIEVANCE INVESTIGATION MEETING

[Date]
[Recipient's Name]
[Recipient's Address]

Dear [ ]

GRIEVANCE LODGED

You are invited to attend an investigation meeting on ____________ at ______________. We are investigating a grievance raised by _______________ on _________________________. The broad nature of the grievance is: _________________________________ [Give an outline of the grievance]. I understand that you may have some information relating to: [list the appropriate points and expand on them as necessary].

- Witnessed events or overheard conversations that may be relevant to the grievance
- Knowledge of the working relationship between _______________________ [Grievant] and ___________________ [Subject of the investigation].
- Useful information concerning the issues that are the subject of the grievance and could assist in conducting the investigation.

Please note that this investigation is a fact-finding exercise. Under the grievance rules for the public service we are obliged to carry out such an investigation. However, we need your assistance to obtain all the facts. Any information you give us will be treated as confidential.

The investigation meeting will be facilitated by: ______________________ and ______________________ will also be present as the transcriber. If you wish, you may be accompanied by a work support person or a union representative of your choice. Please bring with you information / documentation that might be of assistance to the investigation.

If you have any concerns about the grievance investigation, please contact ________________________________ [Contact details]. Alternatively, any concerns that you may have about the process can be raised at the meeting.

As this matter is currently under investigation please keep it confidential.

Thank you for your cooperation. I look forward to hearing from you.

Yours sincerely

Mr. Peter Ramarutsi Raboroko

Signature: ______________________

Chief Executive Officer

Date: ______________________

Types of evidence to collect[4]

It is accepted professional behaviour that decision making in employment matters should be based solely on the facts as they relate to what happened. This includes the evidence received by the investigator, who is suspected, who knows what, and whether any of the parties can substantiate their claims (as required by the rules and law of evidence in South Africa). Stories about dreams and revelations are not acceptable as evidence, since they cannot be subjected to cross-examination in internal processes, or at a labour dispute resolution forum such as the Bargaining Council, the CCMA or the Labour Court.

Sources of evidence, of necessity will have to include the following:

- The complaint form signed by the person alleging sexual harassment.
- Organisational policies as referenced during the investigation.
- Witness interviews as per the investigation plan.
- Email communication or SMS transcripts showing a meeting being called between the parties.
- Physical evidence of inappropriate behaviour showing the alleged harassment, recorded on video or by any other electronic means.

All evidence collected will have to be incorporated in an investigation file compiled by the investigator during the course of the investigation. This investigation file will be kept under lock and key. The same evidence must also show that the investigator complied with the letter and spirit of the terms of reference received from the employer and that there were no irregularities of any kind. As soon as the investigator has completed the investigation process (not the file) he is required to write to the complainant, advising her that the investigation is complete. An example of such a letter is shown below.

Investigation outcome letter to complainant

Asambe National Carriers
19 John Vorster Drive
Kempton Park, Ekurhuleni
0002

PRIVATE AND CONFIDENTIAL
Ms Zubeida Alamein
17 Thatchfield Court
Pretoria
0001

Dear Ms Alamein

RE: OUTCOME OF SEXUAL HARASSMENT COMPLAINT INVESTIGATION

We are writing to let you know the outcome of our investigation. We received your complaint on ______________. After meeting with you to talk about your concerns, we also met with your supervisor ____________________ and certain witnesses. We reviewed all the information and documents gathered in the investigation and have concluded that your complaint is SUBSTANTIATED / NOT SUBSTANTIATED / INCONCLUSIVE (delete whichever is not applicable).

[Include if the complaint is substantiated]: As a result we will be taking steps to make sure that the subject of your concerns does not occur again in the future. For reasons of confidentiality, we cannot tell you all the steps that we will be taking but some of these steps include:

[List actions that are not confidential]: We will follow up with you regarding your general health situation in the coming days in order to find out if there is a need for employee wellness to be involved in the investigation process.

If you are not happy with the outcome of our investigation you can ask that your complaint be reviewed by the Appeal Authority (CEO) by using the Appeal Form in the disciplinary code, or refer the matter to the Bargaining Chamber for the Aviation Industry.

If you have any questions or concerns about our investigation or its outcome, please let us know by contacting Mrs Josephine Mankoeng (HR Director) at (011) 487 1543.

Joe Mbatha (Investigations Manager)

Signature: ____________________

Date: ____________________

Review evidence received and presented[5]

During the course of a workplace investigation, the investigator will come across various types and categories of evidence, including the following:

- Documents (a policy, code, or handbook).
- Witnesses (testifying for or against one of the parties).
- Statutes (including the LRA, 66 of 1995).
- Digital evidence (e-mails, transcripts, etc.).

All of the above pieces of evidence make up a mosaic that will have to be navigated and analysed in order to enable the investigator to assist the decision maker in arriving at a conclusion. Taking everything into account, they will decide whether the allegations have been substantiated, or if there is insufficient evidence to make a decision. This exercise is a factual analysis of what was received and presented to the investigation. The intended outcome of this review of evidence is to:

- Determine the credibility of each one of the witnesses who participated in the interviews conducted by the investigator, based on objective criteria.
- Make findings of fact, as per the above analysis, based on evidence presented by and received from all the witnesses, including the complainant and the subject of investigation.
- Consult with either the internal counsel or external attorneys representing the employer in order to ensure that privileged information is not unwittingly disclosed to a party who is not allowed to receive it, thus exposing the employer to unnecessary risks.

Making conclusions and recommendations[6]

As soon as the received and presented evidence has been analysed and reviewed by the investigator, best practice requires that findings of fact and recommendations be made to the employer. This exercise is a pronouncement by the investigator as to what the options are on the issues that were investigated, as explained under the section above. Procedurally, this process will have to include the following activities:

- The investigator presents an interim report to be forwarded to the complainant, the subject of the investigation, and relevant witnesses asking them to comment on the initial findings.

- In writing, all the above listed persons will be required to comment on the factual findings by a specific date and time, failing which the initial report's findings will be regarded as a true reflection of the facts relating to the issues under investigation.
- By the appointed date, the investigator will revisit the interim report, check if any comments were received, and cross-reference such information with his written notes.
- Simultaneously, the investigator will also be consulting with specialists internally and externally, or relevant investigation team members (as the case may be), in order to ensure that the final report is factually correct.
- On the basis of the completion of the above exercise, the investigator can inform the employer of what has been uncovered by the investigation and make recommendations.

Preservation of collected evidence[7]

Document management within an organisation plays an important role in an investigation. As such, it must be undertaken throughout the process as if in anticipation of litigation. The intention is to reap the benefits of thoroughness whilst simultaneously reducing the potential risks associated with conducting a workplace investigation. To explain:

1. At the beginning of an investigation the investigator is required to commence the investigation using a preliminary investigation plan. Such an investigation plan will list activities relating to the issues to be investigated, based on the terms of reference for that specific investigation. This will be done using a tool known as a table of activities, similar to the one included in Chapter 6.

The plan must be drafted in such a way that it can be used to demonstrate to an alternative dispute resolution forum or a court of law that the employer took prompt corrective action when a complaint was raised and needed to be investigated. This forms part of procedural fairness within the workplace.

2. Document management continues throughout the investigation process, with adjustments and amendments to the plan from time to time. In this regard, witness statements must be collected and recorded as the witnesses are interviewed, factual findings are made and conclusions reached. As a result, a final investigation report is compiled and submitted to the decision makers of the organisation.
3. All of the above activities are managed through an evidence 'chain of custody' document that describes what information was received by the investigation in relation to a particular case. Such a form will also list the date when evidence was received and by whom within the organisation. It will further set out the persons who are entitled to have access to such information, including its disposal, as part of document management.

In a nutshell, the preservation of collected evidence is a central part of ensuring that the employer is able to protect itself against the risks of litigation. It is incumbent on the investigator to ensure that all the information and evidence collected during the process is kept under lock and key for a specified period, as per the investigation protocol. This is then kept in an investigation file which is kept separate from the investigation report, similar to the one in Chapter 5, Box 4.

In summary

Gathering evidence is part of the organisation's investigation methodology – a workplace investigation activity within the plan. It must contribute to achieving a singularly important aspect of legal compliance, namely to show that the employer is only interested in the facts relating to the allegations; nothing more and nothing less.

The facts collected as evidence can either prove that there is a *prima facie* case to be answered by the accused employee, or that there is no factual or legal basis to proceed with the matter at hand and the employee is therefore exonerated. Alternatively, that there is not enough evidence to prove on a balance of probability that misconduct occurred, which means that the employer must abandon the investigation for the time being. This analysis is what is required by procedural fairness in South African labour law. By implication, this means that the employer cannot proceed to the next stage of the inquiry – that is calling a disciplinary hearing – if the evidence cannot show that there is a case to be answered. The employer can only prepare for a disciplinary hearing if there is a list of offences (charge sheet) which are supported by evidence collected during the investigation.

This point is essential, since the employer will be required to prove that it has a case at the disciplinary hearing. This will be the case if and only if it can show through evidence that there are witnesses who can testify to the incidents alleged by the complainant – thus avoiding a 'he said, she said' scenario where it is the word of the complainant against that of the accused.

The employer will need to show that there is physical evidence that can be produced proving that indeed the complainant was harassed by the affected employee. This will be in the form of SMS transcripts, rejected advances, consultations with employee assistance practitioners in order to seek help, and any other tangible sources.

Documentary evidence will need to be produced by the employer, showing that the accused employee is aware of organisational policy relating to harassment as a prohibited behaviour. In addition, the employer is required to produce proof showing that the subject of the investigation received copies of policy documents in person, or electronically.

It is this level of rigorousness that can embolden an employer to proceed to a disciplinary hearing, knowing full well that not even an external labour dispute resolution forum will be able to find against the company, should the accused employee be dismissed by the employer.

GRIEVANCE INVESTIGATION REPORT
CONFIDENTIAL

Investigation into a grievance lodged by: [NAME]

Date: ______________________

Report by: ________________________, Location]

1. DETAILS OF GRIEVANCE

Brief account of main points

____

____

2. INVESTIGATION PROCEDURE

How the grievance was investigated and by whom

____

____

What supporting evidence was provided, by whom and why

____

____

3. FURTHER INFORMATION

Include any other relevant information if applicable – attach letters / meeting notes

____

____

4. CONCLUSION AND RECOMMENDATIONS

Summary of the key points of the report

____

____

Outcome – confirm whether the grievance is upheld, not proved on a balance of probability or inconclusive evidence presented

____

____

____

____

Next steps

____

____

____

____

Training needs

____

____

____

____

5. SUPPORTING DOCUMENTATION

Complete list in a separate file (attached)

Signature: ____________________

Print Name: ____________________

CONSTITUTING AN INVESTIGATION FILE

1. Letter of appointment as an investigator
2. Terms of reference received from CEO
3. Letter notifying employee as subject of investigation
4. Letter inviting employee to investigation meeting
5. Complaint form received and signed by complainant
6. Clear statement of allegations to be investigated
7. List of all involved parties – investigation team members
8. Documents and evidence reviewed
9. Facts uncovered
10. Analysis of facts
11. Recommendations and conclusions reached
12. Correspondence between investigator and parties
13. Administrative action taken (if any), e.g. suspension
14. Interview notes – supporting documentation

Chapter 8

Involving Law Enforcement Services[1]

Organisational policy. Gross Misconduct

"A mandate given to a workplace investigator is not written in stone. Sometimes, it requires clarification, and it evolves as the process unfolds."

- Canadian Broadcast Corporation

Introduction

In workplace investigations, the decision to refer a matter that has been brought to the employer's attention as a potential crime to the SAPS, or any other crime fighting institution, is fraught with both risks and opportunities. The risk relates to the possibility of the suspects withdrawing into a laager. If they are part of organised crime syndicate they may shield collaborators at work and outside, for fear of reprisals. On the other hand, the situation presents the employer with an opportunity to encourage the employee to cooperate for the sake of receiving a potentially lesser sentence if found guilty by a court of law. This is, of course, a separate matter from what happens at the workplace disciplinary hearing, which is an eventuality that cannot be avoided.

There are both advantages and disadvantages for the employer when involving the police in workplace investigations. Any decision as to when and how to involve the crime fighting institutions requires looking into the costs as well as the benefits, both in the short and long term. It requires an ability to be both strategic and tactical in defence of the interests of the employer. It goes almost without saying that the decision will undoubtedly impact the organisation legally, financially, as well as in terms of its reputation.

Private Sector Businesses and Public Sector Organisations[2]

All entities that are registered to do business in South Africa are governed by laws and regulations administered by the DTI and the Treasury, among others. Businesses are required to report all crimes perpetrated by employees and managers to law enforcement agencies. The same rules are applicable to government departments and associated agencies that are required by law, as well as public and social policy, to combat crimes against their clients, employees and citizens. There are no exceptions. All employer organisations, irrespective of their areas of operation, are required to comply with reporting requirements on occupational health and safety laws, as well as general employment laws, except where they are expressly exempted or are excluded by proclamation.

If an employer suspects criminal wrongdoing during an investigation, it is advisable that they involve the SAPS as soon as practically possible.

The rationale for involving law enforcement[3]

Many employer organisations across different sectors have some guidelines, policy or protocol to guide their management of a workplace investigation. Such documents deal with matters that are either specifically employment-related, or matters where criminal activity is suspected.

For instance, in the public service in South Africa the Disciplinary Code and Procedure for the Public Service is a collective bargaining agreement signed between the State as employer and the recognised trade unions, known as PSCBC Resolution 1 of 2003 of this agreement states that: "If an employee commits misconduct that is also a criminal offence, the criminal procedure and the disciplinary procedure will continue as separate and different proceedings."

In addition, the LONMIN[4] Policy on Fraud Investigation states that:

"If the allegation is a crime, which could lead to a criminal prosecution, it will be necessary to involve the police. However, the investigation should not be delayed and any decision to dismiss need not wait for the decision of a criminal court. Therefore, full investigation by the employer is essential and the police should not be asked or relied upon to conduct the investigation on behalf of the employer as there is a different burden of proof."

The two documents referenced here are merely samples of investigation protocols.

Of course, each employer organisation will have a similar set of guidelines on how to address workplace misconduct that is also criminal behaviour; these are for illustrative purposes only. They reflect similarities between the private and public service sectors.

It is important for the employer to take advice from the provisions of its policy or any organisational documents that are applicable when it must conduct a similar workplace investigation. These documents often reference examples of good practice within that sector or industry to be followed in order to avoid allegations of complicity in a crime from a regulator, a relevant state department, or the SAPS.

The decision to involve law enforcement agencies during a workplace investigation must be taken in consultation with that organisation's legal advisor (or attorney of record). The advisor should be knowledgeable about general workplace crimes committed by employees in the course of their duties at work, or outside employment.

The actual timing of when to involve law enforcement agencies is dependent on a number of different factors. These factors include the issues involved, the analysis of potential risk to the investigation (as per the plan), as well as the actual objective of the employer in investigating. It is important that the employer strike whilst the iron is still hot, if it is to achieve the desired results of combating financial and economic crime within organisations.

Aligning Workplace and Criminal Law Investigation Processes[5]

In order to contribute towards combating economic crimes such as corruption, grand theft, bribery and fraud, it is necessary that there be cooperation between employer organisations and the police. It is a battle that cannot be won with one entity marching left and the other one going to the right. Tactically, the parties can march separately (different investigations) whilst striking together (combating financial misconduct as a partnership).

During a workplace investigation, when an employee is suspected of any of the above crimes, it is recommended that the employer consider necessary administrative action (transfer or suspension) in order to protect its organisational interests. Of course, any such action will have to be taken in conformity with the provisions of the employer's disciplinary code and procedures, or its policy on employment relations.

At the same time, the employer can inform the SAPS of a suspected crime. This is to allow the SAPS to commence with their own investigation, without hindrance from the employer. The employer acknowledges that the two processes (the SAPS investigation and an internal workplace investigation) are separate and distinct, yet complimentary. The reason for the separation is the different laws that govern each entity's actions – even though they seek to achieve the same goal. It is even possible for the affected employee to be found guilty during the workplace investigation, but receive a not guilty verdict in a criminal court of law, due to various factual and legal considerations.

One such reason is that the test to determine guilt at a workplace disciplinary hearing is less strict because the outcome is informed by the principle of guilt on a 'balance of probability'. The test to determine guilt in a criminal court of law is based on a stricter standard of proof, which requires an accused person to be found guilty of a crime 'beyond reasonable doubt'.

Nevertheless, the key point to be made is that the employer must always present relevant evidence emanating from the investigation, in order to show the affected employee that there is a case to be answered. This is meant to encourage him to cooperate, while taking care not to make any promises that the allegations may disappear.

The employer must consistently comply with procedural fairness requirements while investigating. This is done in order to avoid unfair dismissal allegations later, when the time to take a decision to dismiss an employee arrives. This approach is a sure guarantee that even if the workplace dispute goes to an external labour dispute resolution forum the employer will win the case, having complied with the requirements of a legal investigation.

A Strategy to Investigate Workplace Fraud

According to Donald Cressey[6], those amongst us who commit fraud in the workplace and in society in general, do so based on a theoretical triangle. This "fraud triangle" consists of: motivation, opportunity and rationalisation.

When employees are involved in activities such as bribery, misrepresentation of facts, theft of employer property, or embezzlement of third-party assets, they show that:

1. They are either motivated by greed or a desire to accumulate wealth by any means necessary. Usually, this is done to improve their social standing as individuals or as a household.
2. An opportunity presented itself, in the form of an employer that has weak internal controls. This enabled them to abuse their positions of power and make decisions that are to the financial detriment of the organisation, by committing financial misconduct or crime.
3. Such crooks and fraudsters attempt to justify their behaviour. They claim that it was necessary, or that it was a victimless crime since no actual persons (as opposed to an organization) became their victim.

It is very important that a workplace investigator who is qualified in the field and familiar with the characteristics of fraud be appointed to conduct the investigation.

Any organisational response to fraud by means of a workplace investigation must consider the above analysis.

Workplace practitioners must take note that fraud is an exceptionally complex act of misconduct. To start with, it is planned carefully as a scheme, by largely senior and executive management in the organisation. So, when the culprits execute the fraud plan, it will be informed by their professional training and practical knowledge of how the internal systems work. International research has also shown that fraud is committed by professionals in finance and procurement, law and project management, as well as those staff members with long years of service as employees. However, the activities are generally undertaken by subordinates, knowingly or unwittingly. Herein lays the conundrum for an organisation that is planning a strategic response. What is to be done?

Tactically, the investigator will have to:

1. Begin the investigation as soon as he receives a complaint that there is a possibility of financial misconduct, relating to procurement of goods and services or a rigged tender, by fully debriefing the complainant and analysing the issues involved.
2. Evaluate the allegations or suspicions to determine factually and legally which allegations of potential financial misconduct can be listed for investigation.
3. Conduct the due diligence and background checks on the suspected internal employees as well as the external parties that are allegedly involved in the fraudulent transactions, using documents and interviews to gather information and evidence.
4. Speedily begin the external investigation by briefing law enforcement agencies and seeking their collaboration with the workplace investigation, in order to avoid a duplication of efforts and a waste of resources.
5. Simultaneously apply for the freezing of assets, whilst proceeding with the investigation.
6. Seek the cooperation of an internal witness who purportedly benefitted less as a result of their position in the organisation. They might be willing to act as a whistle-blower who can testify against the principal perpetrators.

7. Plan to deal with the ringleader in the last leg of the investigation, when enough evidence has been collected to confront them. Seek admissions of guilt or confessions to bring the investigation to finality.

The rationale for the above approach is based on a principle that when investigating financial misconduct, different objectives require different tactics.

In summary

Involving the SAPS, Hawks, NDPP and other related law enforcement agencies in combating financial misconduct in the private sector and public service workplaces is an acknowledgement that financial crimes committed by employees are a priority in South Africa today.

Over the past decade and more we have seen on TV screens, heard over the radio, and read in newspapers what the impact of financial misconduct has been on government departments. Government departments that must deliver public services to citizens, and businesses that must produce consumer services and products. Insiders across all levels and sectors take liberties with funds and assets they were never allowed to have access to by their rightful owners. It is against this backdrop that this chapter was written.

There is both an employment law imperative, as well as a public and social policy requirement, that all the labour market stakeholders are motivated, mobilised and encouraged to participate in a workplace campaign to combat financial misconduct as a societal scourge.

This book contains all the necessary tools, guidelines and strategies on how to deal with financial misconduct as social partners of employers, government and trade unions. A partnership approach is a requirement if society is to achieve a better life for all citizens.

MISTAKES TO AVOID WHEN CONDUCTING WORKPLACE INVESTIGATIONS

1. Failing to initiate an investigation (contrary to Item 4(1) of the *Code of Good Practice: Dismissal*).
2. Not acting promptly, as dictated by good practice or policy / law.
3. Poor selection of the investigation team (EE compliant, with appropriate skills).
4. Lack of objectivity, to avoid bias and tainted findings / recommendations.
5. Failing to investigate thoroughly and then arriving at questionable findings which pose a legal threat to the business.
6. Unprofessional interviews during the investigation (not applying best practice).
7. Not taking accurate or sufficient notes (business approach).
8. Ignoring credibility of witnesses – not checking for collusion or intimidation.
9. Tipping off the affected person, mobbing and ganging up against complainant.
10. Failing to document thoroughly, affecting the credibility of evidence tested by court of law, no physical or digital evidence.
11. Failure to create a detailed report and findings supported by an investigation file.
12. Putting employee privacy ahead of employer needs (complying with POPI and related legislation; defending legal and legitimate interests of employer).
13. Failure to monitor the workforce (managing employment relationship through tools, practice guides and engagement forums).

14. Allowing retaliation against complainant and witnesses (building a civilised workplace).
15. Not following up after completion of investigation (checking that changes are implemented).

Chapter 9

Writing the Investigation Report

Factual findings. Recommendations

"The investigation report should be succinct and clear. It must outline the authorisation, scope and purpose of the investigation; detail the complaint and set out the allegations; outline if on the balance of probabilities each allegation is capable or not of substantiation and include relevant attachments."

- Managing Workplace Investigations:
A Practical Guide for the Queensland Public Sector

Introduction

There are different types of workplace investigation reports. On the one hand, there is the 'simple' report compiled after an investigation that involved a single complainant – one category of offence, like insubordination, and no more than one witness. On the other hand, an investigator can be given the responsibility of performing a complex investigation. For instance, there may be multiple complainants in an 'executive abuse of power' claim against a person who holds a powerful position. This type of investigation can involve up to four accusers and multiple witnesses who are specific to each allegation against the affected person. The investigator will then have to write a report for each one of these cases based on the scope and purpose of the investigation. The final report must be objective and impartial.

Not one single report will have the same 'structure[1]' as another one. Still, in each one of these reports the investigator is required to show the reader of the report what has been done since the beginning of the investigation. This involves listing the persons who were interviewed in order to get information and facts relating to the allegations, referencing the evidence that was collected, and proving or disproving the allegations made by the complainant against the affected person(s).

Generally, writing the investigation report signals that the investigation is complete and that all the basic requirements have been dealt with. It is the penultimate activity in the investigation plan. As a legal document that either exonerates or puts the accused person in a corner, the report must be handled very delicately. The risk is that the same report can be discovered at a labour dispute resolution forum or at a court of law, upon the showing of good cause by the subject of the investigation. So, it must be aligned with the contents of an investigation file (a separate document), which proves that indeed an investigation was conducted.

More importantly, this document must inform the reader of the report of the exact nature of the conduct under investigation – is it sexual harassment, grand theft, abuse of power, or any other workplace misdemeanour. The report should clearly state the parties involved in the drama, as well as which functions and polices of the organisation were affected, prompting the investigation. Lastly, the report must show the time, date and location of all the events relating to the matters under investigation. It is to be supplemented by 'documents[2]' presented at a decision making meeting of the employer, or at a disciplinary hearing.

The chronological story[3]

As a narrative, the investigation report is written to tell and show the reader what happened. This requires an overview of who was involved, where and how the occurrences took place, when the events happened, and why the organisation took a decision to start an investigation. When writing the report, the investigator must list the sequence of events as they unfolded – before, during and after the actual investigation. Anything included has to be proven on a balance of probability, through evidence.

For the investigator to be able to demonstrate that a legally compliant investigation was undertaken, his analysis of evidence relating to the various parts of the investigation must speak to the following ten key aspects, namely:

1. Understanding the complaint

- This intellectual exercise involves the investigator showing in the report that he has the necessary skills and experience as a result of his having dealt with similar issues previously. Hence, the correct classification of the complaint.
- Such classification must also show whether the matter relates to misconduct, an employee grievance against a management decision relating to the interpretation of terms and conditions of employment, or an alleged breach of public / social policy.

2. The decision to investigate

- The report must show that the decision was informed by a preliminary analysis of issues which proved that there is a *prima facie* case of sexual harassment, fraud or other type of misconduct to be investigated by the employer.
- It must also show that the informal approach of managing

workplace disciplinary matters (corrective discipline) will not suffice in this instance, as the allegations are too serious, or that the affected person is a repeat offender who had been counselled previously.

3. Compliance with the investigation policy and protocols[4]

- The investigator perused relevant guidelines which showed the procedure to be followed in order to conduct a thorough workplace investigation.

4. Appointing an investigator

- The employer's decision maker considered the legal issues involved when deciding whether to appoint an internal practitioner or a specialist professional with the rare skills needed in order to handle the specific case (e.g. abuse of executive authority).
- This is to be based on a table of activities showing the start date of the investigation, the planned completion date, as well as the activities planned in order to drive the investigation process until completion.

5. A communication plan[5]

- A plan has been developed to keep in contact with both the complainant and respondent in order to report on work in progress.
- This plan has been designed to update witnesses, managers and all involved parties about any developments, including when the process is stalled by barriers.
- It is governed by the 'need to know' communication principle.

6. Prove that the employer is caring[6]

- The investigation may be adversarial and cause stress for the affected employee. Therefore, the services of employee wellness should be available on a confidential and voluntary basis if they are needed by an employee in distress.

7. The investigator is a law-abiding professional

- The investigator complies with the advice of *Code of Good Practice: Dismissal* in Schedule 8 of the LRA regarding the need for procedural fairness in workplace matters.
- He adheres to the employees' right to be heard by interviewing all the parties before making any recommendations to the employer.
- He ensures that the accused employee is notified that he is the subject of an investigation; in writing, in a language he understands, as required by good practice
- The investigator will ensure that the employee is given an official opportunity to respond to allegations.
- The outcome of the investigation was communicated, in the form of a summary. The employee is asked to confirm that there was an investigation which investigated the facts only.

8. The employer is advised of the findings

- The employer is informed of the findings through a final report compiled as per the scope and purpose set out for the investigation.

9. Findings of the investigation

- Findings are communicated through the conclusion reached by investigator.

10. Manage the aftermath[7]

- Engage with decision makers and all the parties involved on how to do things differently in order to manage employment relations at the workplace and avoid similar incidents in the future. This is done by suggesting an improvement plan to improve organisational culture going forward.

Analysis of Evidence

Every workplace investigation report should have a section where it is shown that all evidence received and presented during the process was carefully analysed. This activity must be factored into the investigation plan. This is standard practice internationally, across all the jurisdictions researched. The evidence to be analysed could include witnesses, documentary items and a list of physical objects collected, among others.

Without an analysis of the above evidence it will be unprocedural (possibly even illegal) to make findings of fact or law. Furthermore, the investigator will not be able to reach a decision on whether to tell the employer if the allegations are substantiated, unsubstantiated or inconclusive.

All the evidence collected, received or presented must be analysed. Depending on the type of investigation – complex or ordinary – the analysis of evidence in the investigation report must:

- Acknowledge the position of both the complainant and the respondent.
- Seek to weigh the facts discovered, regardless of whether there are only two or multiple parties involved.
- Describe the evidence of each presented position in order to conclude whether it is substantiated, unsubstantiated or inconclusive.

- Identify the relevant facts that allowed the investigator to make this determination.
- Analyse and discuss the relevant facts presented by the parties in support of their respective cases.
- Assess the credibility of each witness, in instances where there is a dispute of the facts, by referencing objective factors.
- Allow the investigation report to be able to say which policy, law, prescript or collective agreement has not been complied with, without expressing an opinion on the matter.

In summary

Writing, presenting and communicating an investigation report is an enormous task and difficult to accomplish. It is one of the essential professional skills to be taught to investigators who wish to be legally compliant. This report is the tool that will determine whether the employer has a winnable case that justifies the dismissal of an employee.

Practice Guide

MODEL INVESTIGATION CASE FILE

Letter notifying affected party of date of investigation

Clear statement of allegations / issues to be investigated

Applicable organisational policies

List of all involved parties

Documents and evidence reviewed

Facts uncovered

Analysis of facts

Conclusions reached

Recommendations to organisation

Chapter 10

Managing the Investigation Aftermath

Manage the aftermath. Improve culture

"An investigation is essential, but [it is] not a panacea."

- Worklogic[1]

Introduction

Managing the aftermath of a workplace investigation is not like normal workplace activity. It is also not comparable to attending a dinner party where the host and guests are generally expected to be civil to each other because they are friends. It is more like having to mediate between rival siblings who believe that they are entitled to certain privileges based simply on who they are. This is particularly the case where the respective parties are conscious of their rights, duties, and responsibilities based on their perceived status.

When one of the parties to this employment relationship has had his ego affected by serious allegations of impropriety (regardless of the outcome), the workplace is likely to be affected by his emotions; especially feelings of anxiety, anger, and hurt. This is human nature and is therefore considered normal behaviour.

The other employees, who supported the complainant and the accused (consciously or unconsciously) before, during and after the investigation will likely take sides. Even though the employer can claim that it conducted a legally compliant investigation, it must still address 'how the parties or their supporters relate[2]' after the completion of the investigation. This is where the conundrum lies.

An employer's failure to heal the rift caused by an acrimonious sexual harassment investigation may lead to an unstable workplace. This situation is not beneficial for any of the parties involved. Consider for a moment a situation where the trigger for the complaint that was investigated was a lack of knowledge regarding policies regulating professional conduct in the workplace. It then becomes incumbent on the employer to commence training for all employees in order to ensure they are informed that sexual harassment is prohibited workplace behaviour that is punishable by disciplinary measures, including termination of employment. It is strongly advised that managing the aftermath includes inviting managers and staff to participate in a dialogue to find solutions that are acceptable to all.

Preparation and retention of documents relevant to the investigation

It is standard practice for a workplace investigation report to be constituted of evidence that either shows the allegations to be substantiated, unsubstantiated or inconclusive. This investigator analysis will be arrived at by means of referencing relevant organisational policies, applicable laws, a code of conduct with rules of acceptable behaviour, and a contract of employment review. Last mentioned will include a collective bargaining agreement that guides the employer on how to manage misconduct or address an alleged breach of workplace guidelines.

The collecting and safely storing of workplace investigation documents is integral to the writing of a final investigation report. Without the documents listed above, there can be no legitimate or legal report to assist the employer while in pursuit of justice.

This essential activity is undertaken at the beginning of the investigation, immediately after a potential violation of workplace rules is reported to the organisation. It continues during the investigation when the investigator complies with procedural fairness by writing to the participants, informing them of the investigation underway and inviting them to a meeting in order to get the facts.

The key documents to be collected during the investigation will include the witness statements, dated interview notes, electronic and physical evidence, and recordings of interviews. The employer information management strategy will also have guidelines on how to store all this information in anticipation of any future legal disputes.

The document management system will clearly state the names of those team members with access to the documents collected as evidence, on a need to know basis. It may even restrict access to certain parts of the documents in order to safeguard information that is crucial to the investigation. This is to maintain the confidentiality and credibility of the investigation, as per the policy.

All the above documents will have to be kept under lock and key, and generally be accessed only by the investigator who will offer them as attachments when the final report is presented.

Practice Guide

SECURITY FOR INVESTIGATION FILES AND RECORDS

Maintain a separate investigation file containing:

1. All interview notes
2. All communication with witnesses
3. All written statements
4. All documents that support / refute the allegation(s)
5. The investigation report
6. Any recorded statements and transcripts
7. Relevant organisational policies
8. Applicable laws and collective agreements
9. Letters to affected persons and third-party witnesses
10. Letter of appointment as investigator
11. Investigation terms of reference
12. Letters to the complainant (internal / external)

Adapted from, *Oregon State Government Investigation Toolkit.*

Levels of intervention[3]

An organisation seeking to rebuild relationships of trust after an investigation will have to bring all the workplace parties on board. This means engaging the affected individuals, their teams, and the organisation as a whole.

In this regard, the suggested interventions can include activities such as:

- Mediating[4] between the individuals – the complainant and the accused during the investigation (if both parties agree to this as a viable solution).
- Having one-on-one meetings between the complainant and the accused about designing a way forward, if they are still employed by the organisation.
- Encouraging management to attend coaching[5] and capacity building initiatives. This will help them acquire skills to better manage the employment relationship, by identifying incorrect behaviour and discouraging it before it becomes misconduct.
- Promoting team building[6] within a division to ensure that there is agreement on the roles of all the parties concerned, regardless of status at the workplace.
- Facilitating discussions between the team members where the investigation is explained, including the lessons received by the organisation.
- Promoting compliance with best practice relating to the management of the employment relationship.

In summary

It is required that the major intervention be the implementation of an improvement philosophy encompassing the entire organisation. This philosophy should not only seek to identify the root causes of the trigger that led to the complaint, but also pre-empt its recurrence in the future. This forms a comprehensive response to a situation that requires real leadership.

Practice Guide

FUNDAMENTALS OF CONDUCTING AN EMPLOYMENT INVESTIGATION

- Identify the issues to be investigated.
- Determine who should be advised of the complaint / grievance and the need to investigate.
- Consider the implications of union involvement, in a unionised workplace.
- Determine whether the investigation should be privileged and take the steps required to maintain the applicable legal privilege.
- Consider the timetable for the investigation.
- Consider how the investigation should be documented.
- Identify the sources of information to be reviewed.
- Determine the order in which information should be sought.
- Determine which witnesses to interview including the themes to be covered.
- Determine what disclosures must be made to the interviewee and whether the interviewee's attorney must or should be permitted at the interview.
- Determine who should attend the interviews.
- Prepare a statement to be made at the beginning of the interviews.
- Prepare to deal with the employee who fails to cooperate.
- Determine the consequences of an employee's failure to cooperate.
- Consider implementing temporary remedial measures while the investigation is continuing.

Adapted from *Workplace Investigations: The Initial Investigation Planning Checklist ABA Section of Labour and Employment Cle Conference*

Chapter 11

Competence Building to Mainstream Workplace Investigations[1]

Targeting financial and legal risks by identifying; analysing and managing employment issues before they escalate into disputes

"Training in conducting internal investigations covers both the legalities of the process as well as best practices. It gives practitioners confidence to address allegations of misconduct, harassment, theft and to conduct employee investigations without fear of reprisal or legal exposure for conducting the workplace investigation."

- HR Training Centre

Introduction

The training of practitioners in the basics of conducting legally compliant workplace investigations must be understood as a societal necessity, not a luxury that can be dispensed with when an employer is faced with budgetary constraints. This activity is one of the key requirements for pursuing justice at work while managing the employment relationship. Therefore, training is the best way to ensure that South Africa will plant the seeds for the growth of a solid workplace investigation community[2]. Eventually, this body of professionals will contribute to the development of accredited qualifications that can improve a practitioner's prospects of advancement as a professional in a new, but internationally recognised field of expertise.

In this regard, it is worth mentioning that there are too many professionals with HR or employment law qualifications, who still have no professional competency or experience relating to investigating acts of misconduct or poor work performance. These professionals draft the all important 'charge sheet' which determines the fate of employed people; people who later end up being unfairly dismissed due to a lack of investigatory skills on the part of employer representatives. The same situation applies with operational managers and supervisors who do not manage the employment relationship as contractually expected, but rather allow HR / ER practitioners to take over their duties. This even extends to the informal approach to investigating before applying the corrective disciplinary processes.

The professional acquisition of investigatory skills will ensure that workplace investigators are elevated to a level equivalent to fraud examiners[3] and other investigators in the country – professionally trained individuals with specialised knowledge. This would be a great achievement as it would mean that workplace transformation campaigns directed at financial misconduct, harassment and victimisation could be accelerated in both the public service and the private sector (as noted in Chapter 8).

It is disappointing that a preliminary investigation into what is currently happening in the field of workplace investigations reveals that we have a 'limited choice of South African training courses'[4] or training programmes that are informed by the *Code of Good Practice: Dismissal* in Schedule 8 of the LRA, 66 of 1995.

Given the fact that there are no accredited professional training programmes in South Africa, we have no choice but to borrow from 'international jurisdictions'[5], instead of attempting to reinvent the wheel. So where do we begin? In light of the above analysis, we must begin where we are.

Capacity-building and training methodology[6]

With specific reference to the pedagogy of professional capacity building, we must accept that we are starting at ground zero on the subject. As previously indicated, the basics of learning and teaching about conducting a workplace investigation should be approached as a combination of theory and practice. In this respect, it is proposed that Australian, Doug Malouf's empowerment model, known professionally as the Tell / Show / Do / Review[7] approach to learning and teaching, be used.

In this section we discuss a tried and tested method of training professionals. It differs from the norm, where standardised information sessions could make practitioners feel as though they are inexperienced students in a classroom. As with building a sturdy house, it is important to start by laying a solid foundation when attempting to transform the capacity building and training methodology on conducting workplace investigations in South Africa.

This foundation will have to be made up of case studies (often relayed through anecdotes), examples, illustrations, demonstrations, facts, and statistics. Together these components will form the framework for theory and practice to interact with each other. Such an approach is guaranteed to stand the test of time, regardless of the type or content of the training.

While delivering any training programme about this subject matter, the facilitator will have to ensure that:

- Course participants are kept alert through information sessions, electronic media and group work.
- The pace of presentation is varied, depending on the exercise conducted at the time.
- Participants are involved as active learners.
- Different learning tools are applied as teaching aids, including humour and storytelling.

- The capacity-building process is learner-based and activity-based.
- A message is conveyed by the facilitator; informed by the laws of learning which require that an idea be explained, reinforced and sold as beneficial to the learner.
- Each module is characterised by five must-know statements that are summarised as key words, to convey a mental picture of the subject.

A typical design of a basic training programme will look like the one suggested in the table.

Training initiative: conducting workplace investigations			
Tell	Show	Do	Review
This is the theoretical aspect, where a case study on potential general misconduct is presented to the participants.	The facilitator shares with the participants the skills of conceptualisation, design, and execution of an investigation.	The facilitator further breaks the class up into different study groups with a reporter and transcriber as leaders.	Each group or team is required to present their view of the case study.
It is about delivery of information, on how to do things, e.g. how to investigate.	This is an explanation or a demonstration of a skill such as the 7 Steps of Conducting a Legally Compliant Workplace Investigation. It must follow the process flow chart.	This session is about problem-solving and an opportunity to practice skills. Different groups of participants explain each step based on their own understanding of it.	An assessment of skills acquired during the training should be done. Was there a transfer from the facilitator to the participants? Criticism and self- criticism applies.

The objective is to comply with procedural fairness requirements as per Item 4(1) of the *Code of Good Practice: Dismissal* in Schedule 8 of the LRA, 66 of 1995.	This step requires the participants to apply these skills to a new case study on any topic / matter.	It is a facilitated discussion, based on the five different case studies in the book.	Evaluation of learning and teaching methods for improvement. Determine what needs to be done differently in future. Offer of a professional 'helping hand'.
The facilitator assists by sharing his own skills and experiences with the participants.		The different groups are asked to deal with the case study and report back to an open session.	Participants are expected to critique what they learned while applying the skills the presenter shared with them.

It is important to note that this model differs from other information sessions in that the theoretical training component is balanced with skills practice. With the Doug Malouf approach, there is an acknowledgement that practitioners are professionals and adults. As such, they have acquired some prior knowledge throughout their careers. The approach here is to build on this foundation, improve and supplement in areas where skills are lacking, and thereby introduce new investigation methods.

Participants in a workplace investigation capacity-building course will be trained to improve the following competencies[8]:

1. Personal qualities
2. Knowledge
3. Skills

Participants in these capacity-building courses are trained to build on their previous experiences. The idea is to help participants by teaching them to adapt what works and applying it to their own situation through participating in the training sessions, instead of just passively listening to the facilitator. In this way, there is effective communication between participant and trainer to ensure that they maximise the benefits of the capacity-building programme. Simultaneously, there will be cross-fertilisation[9] of the course, as the past workplace investigation experiences of participants will contribute towards enriching the material for everyone.

Programme built using this approach should make it clear to participants that each investigation has a before, during, and after stage. The nuances of each stage should clearly emerge and the confusion of issues relating to the different stages (conceptualisation, design and planning) should be avoided. Also, be aware of the possible conflation of tasks (execution) during each one of the stages. There is no "Chinese Wall" dividing the same stages as shown in the Table. Each preceding stage will flow into the next one.

The framework for conducting the actual training should be informed by the phases that constitute the *7 Step Best Practice Employment Investigations Platform* included in the Table. In practice, the design of the programmes will have to take into account the level of competency of each group trained, their available time as full time employees, challenges faced in their organisation relating to conducting workplace investigations, and the intended outcomes, as well as the overall objectives of the training. Organisations are encouraged to structure their approach to workplace investigation skills building.

In addition to this, the competence-building initiatives should be integrated into an organisation's overall strategy, management structures and accountability systems. It should be ingrained in the governance system of an employer organisation. Operationally, such a capacity-building programme can include a two-day short course on a strategic issue such as compiling an investigation report, or a course over a full week on the fundamental aspects of conducting a thorough workplace investigation.

Training topics to be included

It is acceptable for training programmes to differ in their conceptualisation, design, objectives and intended outcomes. For instance, a two-day workplace investigation introduction course[10] can have topics such as the following:

1. LRA, 66 of 1995 and the conduct of a workplace investigation.
2. Common elements of an investigation of financial misconduct.
3. When does the employer need to investigate?
4. Understanding the allegations.
5. Seeking the appropriate investigator
6. Designing the misconduct investigation
7. Identifying the witnesses.
8. nterviewing the witnesses.
9. Getting hold of necessary documents.
10. Making findings and recommendations for the final report.

More importantly, a comprehensive five-day employment investigations course[11] could deal with all of the following workplace transformation issues. These are commonly reported as challenges for practitioners:

1. How to investigate general misconduct.
2. How to investigate poor work performance.
3. How to investigate workplace harassment.
4. How to investigate bullying and victimisation.
5. How to investigate discrimination.
6. How to investigate OHS Act accidents.
7. How to investigate abuse of executive authority by a senior manager.

All the above issues and topics are just the beginning of a broad empowerment programme for practitioners. It is then up to each workplace or employer, specific to their industry or sector, to identify the specific issues that impact them. Employer associations as industry representative organisations are better placed to design a training programme as it will be easier for them to know the challenges of their industry.

These two lists of matters on which practitioners should be trained as part of basic and advanced programmes serves as a clarion call to employers to get it right from the beginning. As they say, the journey of a thousand miles begins with one step. Here is that step!

Workplace investigation competencies

The most important person in a simple investigation is the investigator. In a complex investigation it could be a team of investigators that forms the main driver without which the vehicle (employer) cannot move. Consequently, without competent professionals charged with the responsibility of conducting the workplace investigation it will become a damp squib that fails to produce the required results.

An employer aiming to protect its reputation must ensure that it only hires investigators with the right competencies, qualifications and professional experience. As standard practice, all persons classified as workplace investigators must prove to independent observers and employees of their organisation that[12]:

- They can articulate the key principles of managing professional workplace investigations related to natural justice.
- They are familiar with the rights of different parties involved in an investigation.
- They can conceptualise, design and execute an organisational strategy for conducting a workplace investigation.
- They can conduct a meeting about any complaint received or brought to their attention – internally or externally – with the complainant and respondent, respectively, without compromising the employer.
- They can assemble statements from those for or against the parties at the workplace, or anywhere else.
- They can contribute to the execution of a legitimate decision-making process, using the balance of probabilities principle.
- They can make legitimate decisions about the next steps once allegations under investigation are found to have been substantiated.
- They can make legal decisions about what information may be released to the various parties involved in the investigation.

In summary

Analytically, the Tell / Show / Do / Review model of learning and teaching is recommended as an intervention and a professional empowerment tool. In theory, it introduces professionals to a different way of acquiring knowledge in the workplace.

In practice, it shows practitioners how to do things differently, based on their training on using critical decision-making tools to achieve a strategic objective. It further introduces the professionals responsible for advice on the management of the employment relationship to an instrument they can use to assess and mitigate risks by complying with legal prescripts, organisational policy, applicable laws, and workplace collective bargaining agreements.

As a combination of theory and practice, the new training approach suggested here seeks to encourage a more active role for the workplace investigator in organisational decision-making on employment matters.

All workplace investigations training must cover every step of the process. From the point at which an employee initiates a grievance or a manager makes allegations of misconduct or poor work performance, until the matter is resolved. But more importantly, all training should be conducted by qualified, experienced and approachable facilitators. All attempts must be made to avoid boring training sessions participants will find uninteresting and unhelpful.

Comprehensive capacity-building programmes like these are meant for the empowerment of professionals. These courses should help practitioners identify the triggers of workplace investigations and devise tactics to deal with them as an additional risk. It must also impart skills in workplace investigators to ensure they avoid the common mistakes made while conducting employment investigations.

Practice Guide

A BEST PRACTICE EMPLOYMENT INVESTIGATION

1. On receiving the allegations of misconduct / grievance on terms and conditions of employment, decide whether to investigate or not.
2. Take immediate administrative action, if necessary (gross misconduct).
3. Choose an investigator among practitioners, or a team of investigators.
4. Plan the investigation.
5. Conduct interviews.
6. Gather documents and other evidence.
7. Evaluate the collected, received and presented evidence.
8. Act.
9. Document the investigation by making use of a case file.
10. Follow-up to ensure recommendations are implemented.

Chapter 12

Definitions of Key Concepts and Terms

Application and Explanation of specific terminology

"A man's mind, stretched by a new idea, can never go back to its original dimension."

- Oliver Wendell Holmes

Introduction

No authoritative book on conducting legally compliant workplace investigations in South Africa would be complete without a list of the key concepts and terms applied by professional workplace investigators all over the world.

The objective of this chapter is to encourage the creation of a national community of practice that shares a common language, like other professions, such as medical professionals, law, accounting, and auditing practitioners do.

The list of terms and concepts included in this manual is not exhaustive. The goal of the list is to explain the most pertinent terms, as well as a few of the ones most frequently used throughout the book.

Instead of organising the terms by topic or under different headings they are listed alphabetically to enable easy reading and referencing. The terms and concepts listed here form the common language used by practitioners who are charged with the responsibility of conducting a workplace investigation. It is only a structured, professional capacity-building programme that can breathe life into the application and meaning of these concepts.

Advice to the reader: You may want to refer back to this chapter as you read on.

A	
Term	**Definition / Explanation**
Accusation	A claim made by one person / organisation against another person, claiming that a crime or an offence has been committed.
Accuse	To directly and formally institute legal proceedings against a person, claiming that s/he committed an offence or a crime.
Adjourn	Briefly postpone or delay a legal process.
Adjudication	The determination of a legal dispute through the pronouncement of a judgement by a court of law.
Admissible evidence	Evidence received by a court of law or a labour dispute resolution forum in deciding a dispute.
Affected person	An employee who is the subject of a workplace investigation; sometimes called 'the accused'.

Appeal authority	An executive authority with the responsibility to hear employee appeals in respect of workplace matters.
Allegation	A claim or assertion made by one employee against another, or the workplace management, claiming that a term or condition of employment was breached.
Anonymous statement	Allegations made by email, telephone, a letter, or another avenue, without the person identifying themselves.
Arbitration	A process whereby workplace disputes are resolved by referring them to a fair and objective third party known as an arbitrator, who makes a final decision.
Assessing credibility	Analysing the plausibility of a witness's story to check for inconsistencies in evidence, or supporting evidence from other sources that corroborates and supports a particular account by verifying the consistency of witness evidence.
Assessment	The evaluation of an allegation or complaint to determine its credibility, materiality and verifiability. These matters are assessed to determine if there is a legitimate basis that warrants investigation.
Attorney-client privilege	A legal privilege that works to keep confidential communications between a legal representative and the client confidential, in anticipation / preparation for litigation.

Audi alterem partem principle	The universal legal principle stipulating that all accused persons must be accorded the right to state their case in response to allegations made against them as part of their defence, in order to ensure justice.

B	
Term	**Definition / Explanation**
Balance of probabilities test	The standard of proof required in civil law cases, such as workplace matters. It means that, based on the evidence provided, it is more probable than not that what the person says happened is true.
Background investigation	A selection method that attempts to reveal the real nature of the job applicant in terms of character, employment history, academic, and financial history.
Bias	A pre-existing attitude or opinion that favours one side over another in a dispute, while ignoring evidence.
Breach (of terms and conditions of employment)	An act of breaking or failing to observe a law, workplace standard of behaviour, a policy, or code of conduct, including an ethics code.
Burden of proof	The burden to prove what is alleged. In workplace investigation matters this obligation rests on the person or employer representative making the allegations.

C	
Term	**Definition / Explanation**
Case law	The law based on decided cases ruled on by judges in a court of law, or commissioners in a labour dispute resolution forum.
Case file	The investigation file compiled by the investigator, containing all the evidence collected and received.
Case study	A 'true to life' inquiry featuring a subject of the investigation, the complainant, and witnesses, showing how to conduct an investigation.
Circumstantial evidence	Evidence that relies on an inference to connect it to a particular fact, issue, or conclusion. For example; a statement made by the 'accused' advising others of a need to 'deal' with a person who is viewed to be an outsider and therefore a threat to vested interests.
Code of good practice	A set of guidelines for fair practice in a specific sector, developed for general application, a specific industry or profession.
Corroboration	To strengthen or support an allegation through other independent, relevant and reliable evidence.
Complaint / Complainant	A report of unacceptable conduct or illegal actions, including unfair behaviour that is prohibited by employment law, organisational policy, a rule, or standard. Generally the matter is raised by an employee or a client of the employer. The person making the complaint is known as the complainant.

Comply	Adhering to laws applicable to a specific situation, court decisions, regulations, executive orders, policy prescripts, and other legal mandates governing employer action.
Collusion	A secret agreement between two people presenting a united front against another when dealing with a legal situation where their interests converge.
Conclusive evidence	Evidence that is incontrovertible, proving the existence of a *prima facie* case to be answered.
Confidentiality	Protection against disclosure to an outside person, of information revealed in a professional discussion such as an investigation.
Conflict of interest	A situation where a person's own interests or a duty towards someone else may affect the way they carry out a duty towards others.

D	
Term	**Definition / Explanation**
Decision maker	The person appointed to determine the veracity of allegations and complaints. Also, the person charged with taking legally acceptable action in respect of substantiated allegations or complaints.
Direct evidence	Evidence involving sight, hearing, smell, taste or feeling that a witness himself can attest to, without reference to communication with a third party.

Disciplinary code and procedure	A document listing acts of misconduct as defined by the employer, showing the procedure to be followed if and when an employee is suspected or accused by the employer, as per the requirements of procedural and substantive fairness.
Disciplinary investigation	A systematic and fair inquiry conducted by the employer, in respect of a rule violation, policy breach or failure to comply with applicable laws. Generally applies to allegations of serious misconduct.
Disclosure	Giving particular information to another party, as required by a contract or legal process.
Dismissal	Termination of an employment relationship either by an employer on just cause shown, or by an employee through a voluntary resignation.
Documentary evidence (Contract, policy, statement, emails, or photograph.)	Evidence that is mainly useful if testified to by a witness, who says under oath that a document is an original, not a copy; the signature on a document is that of a named person. Weight is normally attached to it, for it to be authoritative / persuasive.
Document management	A management information system undertaken by an investigator at the start of the process, until investigation is completed, showing who will have access to what information, including the procedure for access.

Duty to cooperate	A good faith requirement arising from labour law statutes, requiring employees to assist in an investigation when required to do so by an employer.

E	
Term	**Definition / Explanation**
Electronic evidence	Computers, files, digital communication, instant messages, SMS messages, Facebook, Twitter, Skype, and voice messages.
Employee	A person who is working for another person / organisation called an employer and is entitled to be paid a salary or wages, especially at non-executive level.
Employee handbook	A book given to employees by an employer. It usually includes information about employer culture, policies and procedures to regulate behaviour at work.
Employment laws and rules	BCEA, EEA, LRA, SDA, UIA, and COIDA are all labour laws. Rules include work hours, sick leave, rest periods, as well as relations between management and employees.
Enquiry (disciplinary)	Refers to an internal disciplinary meeting called by the employer, where an employee is presented with a list of allegations of misconduct. Normally conducted in accordance with a code and procedure.

Evidence	Any legitimately obtained and relevant facts or information, or items that tend to prove or disprove a fact material to the investigation, or more generally a complaint including an allegation.
Exculpatory evidence	Evidence that tends to show that the affected person had no intent, or did not commit the alleged act or conduct under investigation.
Exhibits	A paper, document or other article produced and exhibited to a court during a trial, a workplace disciplinary inquiry, or arbitration hearing and on being accepted is marked for identification or admitted in evidence.
Expert witness	A witness who has special knowledge about a certain subject, upon which he will testify. This knowledge is not commonly possessed by the average person.
Eye witness	A person who can testify about a matter because of his own presence at the time of the event.

F	
Term	**Definition / Explanation**
Fact-finding	A determination made by an investigator stating the facts discovered by the investigation.
Financial misconduct	Fraud, corruption, theft, dishonesty or deceit by an employee; inappropriate expenditure of funds; questionable internal controls and failure to comply with accounting standards and audit practises.

Forensic investigation	Gathering and analysing of all crime-related physical evidence in order to come to a conclusion about a suspect in a workplace misconduct case.
Framework	A basic structure underlying a system, concept, or text. Includes a particular set of rules, beliefs or ideas which are used in order to deal with problems or decide what to do.
Fraud	An intentionally dishonest act (or lack of action) done to deceive someone or an organisation.
Frivolous allegation	An allegation made without foundation and which embarrasses or annoys the other party.
G	
Term	**Definition / Explanation**
General misconduct	Acts of misconduct not classified as serious. Includes once-off late coming, not wearing a uniform, leaving work before knock-off time, etc. Can be handled through 'corrective discipline' methods.
Grievance	Any discontent or dissatisfaction arising from a feeling or belief of injustice felt by an employee or a group of employees in connection with their work environment.
Grievance Procedure	A collective agreement negotiated between an employer and a trade union, as a means of internal dispute resolution for employees who are not happy about their terms and conditions of employment.

Gross misconduct	A very serious allegation of a misdemeanour committed by an employee, carrying the possibility of dismissal if found guilty.
Ground rules	Rules of conduct for parties in a workplace forum stating how issues are to be addressed; how each party communicates with its constituency.

H	
Term	**Definition / Explanation**
Hearsay evidence	Evidence of a fact not personally seen or heard by a witness, but testified to by him to have been said by another person. Hearsay evidence is normally not permissible in legal proceedings, save for a few exceptions that are allowed by the rules and law of evidence.
Hostile work environment	A workplace in which unwelcome comments or conduct based on gender, race, religion, sexual orientation or other legally protected characteristics unreasonably interfere with an employee's work performance.

I	
Term	**Definition / Explanation**
Inadmissible evidence	Evidence that cannot be used in legal proceedings, because it was acquired illegally.
Inculpatory evidence	Evidence that shows, or tends to show, a person's involvement in an act, or evidence that can establish guilt.

Information sources (investigation)	Employee handbook, labour laws, employer policies, good practice in a sector or industry.
Insufficient evidence	Evidence which fails to meet the burden of proof, leading to a dismissal of a legal matter by a court of law adjudicator or a dispute resolution commissioner.
Interview	A meeting between an investigator and a party to the investigation, designed to gather information about an incident in order to find the truth. Based on a set of questions.
Interview subject	A narrator in an investigation, talking to the investigator by invitation, as a result of being relevant to the issues being investigated.
Interview notes	A systematic record of facts and circumstances relating to a workplace investigation, showing an allegation or complaint made; a tool used to inform decision makers about what was said in a meeting.
Investigator (workplace)	An appropriately qualified practitioner appointed by the employer to investigate a workplace issue and make recommendations based on the facts arising from an investigation. May be internal or external.
Investigation meeting	An engagement that is coordinated by the investigator, involving all the parties concerned. Intended to discuss who, what, where, when, and why.

Investigation leader	A person, usually a manager who leads an investigation, on behalf of the employer. Prepares the final report for presentation to the employer.
Investigation activities	Actionable plan of activities included in a table, showing what will be done, when, by whom, and where.
Investigation aftermath	A process undertaken by the employer to ensure that all the issues emanating from the process of investigation are addressed by the organisation.
Investigation participant	A person who is not the investigation subject, but who cooperates with an investigation (for example a witness who provides information to investigators).
Involved parties	Affected person, witnesses, investigator, complainant, aggrieved, and decision-maker.

L	
Term	**Definition / Explanation**
Labour organisation	A staff association or trade union representing the interests of its members at work.
Labour Relations Act, 66 of 1995 (South Africa)	An act of parliament that regulates employment relations between employers and employees, including the relationship between organised formations representing employers and workers. It has codes of good practice to guide the parties on specific subjects impacting the workplace.

Law enforcement services (South Africa)	The SAPS and its agencies such as the Hawks which investigate crimes; the NPA that prosecutes persons charged with a crime; and, the judiciary that sentences those found guilty of a crime.
Lay witness	An ordinary person who testifies based upon their personal knowledge and life experiences. Testify to fact and perceptions.
Leading question	A question that prompts or encourages the answer wanted by the person asking.
Labour relations policy	Guidelines which are concerned with the management and regulation of relationships at work, involving an employer and interest groups.
Legal and policy context	Labour laws governing employment in the legal context, informed by the Constitution as supreme law of South Africa. Policy context refers to the public and social policy about fairness at work.
Legal process	The methods by which legal rights are enforced; the specific machinery for carrying on a lawsuit, including processes; pleadings; rules of evidence and rules of legal precedent.
Legal representative's list of witnesses	Witnesses a party wishes to appear on his behalf, excluding themselves as applicant or respondent.

M	
Term	**Definition / Explanation**
Malicious Allegation	False allegations and accusations made against a person, with no basis in fact or in law; with the intention to tarnish the image of the accused person. May lead to a lawsuit against the accuser, for defamation of character.
Manual	A book giving instructions or information on how to do a task; an essential guide to the theory and practice of a profession
Material Witness	A witness whose testimony is likely to be sufficiently important to influence the outcome of a legal process, or proceedings.
Mediation	Intervention in a workplace dispute, in order to resolve it, through a discussion facilitated by a competent labour market professional.
Methodology	A systematic, theoretical analysis and practical application of the techniques, tools and strategies applied to a field of study or a branch of knowledge, e.g. workplace investigation.
Model	A system or procedure used as an example to follow or apply, in order to achieve an objective; includes a letter or a report.
Mitigation circumstances / factors	Any information or evidence regarding the circumstances surrounding the offence that might result in a lesser outcome.

N	
Term	**Definition / Explanation**
Need to know	Requiring that only those individuals who must have access to be able to carry out their jobs or have other strong justification for seeing the information, should be provided access.

O	
Term	**Definition / Explanation**
Offence	A list of prohibited acts of behaviour, as per a workplace code of conduct or disciplinary code.
Outcome and letter	A determination made by the investigator, saying whether the investigation substantiated the allegations, failed to substantiate claims or there was insufficient evidence. This is communicated in writing and is called an outcome letter.
Oral proof	Testimony given verbally by a witness, under oath at internal workplace investigation.

P	
Term	**Definition / Explanation**
Perjury	The offence of wilfully telling an untruth or making a misrepresentation under oath, as a witness.
Person responsible	In a workplace investigation, the person who has been assigned a task, as per the investigation plan.

Physical evidence	Real evidence that can be testified to by a witness. A material object that plays some role in the matter that triggered the investigation.
Poor work performance allegations	An alleged failure by the employee to reach and maintain the employer's work performance standards, in terms of quality and quantity of output.
Practitioner	A person actively engaged in an art, discipline or profession. Someone involved in a skilled job or activity whose regular work has involved considerable training and/or study.
Preliminary analysis / assessment	An activity undertaken at the beginning of an exercise / project in order to determine the key issues including what is to be done to activate a process such as an investigation.
Prescripts	An ordinance, law or guidance; a rule or regulation of conduct in a workplace.
Prima facie case	A matter that can be proved, based on the first impression of facts received, obtained or presented; remains as such, until rebutted by a set of contrary facts.
Process of investigation	A theoretical approach, explaining how the investigation was authorised, what evidence was collected, the persons interviewed and statements received, including the outcome.

Privileged information	Legally protected communication between parties to a legal process, such as an investigation. Such information cannot be disclosed unless so directed by a court of law during the course of litigation.
Procedural fairness	Legal procedure informed by the rules of natural justice; to be followed by a workplace decision-maker to ensure that an accused person is able to present his case in defence of the allegations levelled against him.

Q	
Term	**Definition / Explanation**
Question of fact	An explanation of what actually happened in a situation or event between parties to a dispute.
Question of Law	A question that must be answered by applying relevant legal principles, to enable the interpretation of a law(s).

R	
Term	**Definition / Explanation**
Rebuttal	A statement claiming that a point is factually incorrect by providing proof to the contrary. For example, evidence presented by a witness.
Recommendations	A suggestion or proposal as to the best course of action. Often put forward by a person with authority, such as an investigator.

Records of interviews	A list of evidence showing that parties were interviewed, including typed or handwritten minutes, audio, Skype conversations, and telephone recordings.
Report of investigation	An investigation narrative that forms the basis of any future action on issues that were investigated; a clear and unambiguous statement on and analysis of the facts uncovered by the investigator, as mandated by the employer.
Representative	A person who is appointed to speak on behalf of an employee during an investigation at work.
Resources	HR / ER professionals who are professionally competent to investigate; internal security staff who are similarly qualified; internal legal advisors or external counsel; third party professionals with experience on a subject matter.
Respondent	The person against whom a complaint or an allegation is made.
Retaliation	When an employer punishes an employee for engaging in a legally protected activity, relating to duties, rights and responsibilities at work. It can include negative job action, such as illegal demotion, unwarranted disciplinary action, salary reduction, transfers, and mobbing. It can also be very subtle and difficult to detect.
Regulatory framework (investigations)	Employer policies and known industry standards; contract of employment; common law duties; public and social policy guidelines and labour laws.

Right to representation	A natural justice requirement to ensure that employees can (if they so wish) be defended when accused and investigated by the employer.
Right not to incriminate oneself	A right that is protected by Section 35 of the Constitution. It protects persons from making statements that can expose themselves to being charged with potential offences and crimes during an investigation.
Risks of an investigation	Legal, financial and reputational factors that need to be considered during the planning stages of the investigation.
Rule of law	The restriction of the arbitrary exercise of power by subordinating it to well-defined and established laws of a country.

S	
Term	**Definition / Explanation**
Single point of accountability (SPA)	The office that is charged with the ultimate responsibility of deciding the way forward after an investigation. It can be the lead investigator or the accounting officer.
Scope and purpose (investigation)	Boundaries of an investigation; informed by the terms of reference provided by the employer. Used as the basis for the final report.
Sources of evidence	Documents, witnesses, subject matter, experts.
Standard practice	The usual method used by a profession, or branch of knowledge.

Statement	A written declaration made by a person, testifying under oath to what he knows. Must be signed by a witness to be admissible in legal proceedings.
Substantiated facts	Facts that have been verified as correct; they support a claim made by a party to the investigation.
Supporting documents	List of all actions and communications regarding the investigation, by date; constitutes the case file.
Support person	Someone nominated by the employee to attend an investigation meeting with them in order to provide emotional support and reassurance.

T	
Term	**Definition / Explanation**
Template	A pre-designed 'how to' document, crafted as a guide to accomplish a task such as letter writing, report writing, or interviewing witnesses.
Terms of reference	A detailed guide for the investigator, on how to investigate. Sets out the issues to be investigated, possible timeframes, policies and laws to be referenced, including methodology.
Testify	Acting as a witness in an investigation.
Transcript	A complete, written copy of spoken or written words from a meeting. Based on a recording.

U	
Term	**Definition / Explanation**
Unfair labour practice	An unfair act or omission that arises between an employer and employee relating to prohibited activities that can be construed as an injustice by the employee.
Unsubstantiated allegations	Statements made by a person, making claims without providing facts to back them up.
V	
Term	**Definition / Explanation**
Vexatious allegation	Allegations without evidence, or insufficient facts to prove that an accusation is true.
Vicarious liability	A groundless complaint made with an adverse primary intent to cause distress, detriment or harassment to the subject.
Victimisation	Punishing or threatening to punish an employee because he is, for example, assertive; knows his workplace rights; is not part of the inner decision-making circle, etc.

W	
Term	**Definition / Explanation**
Whistle-blower	A person who exposes any kind of information or activity that is deemed illegal, unethical or unacceptable within either the private or public sector.

Witness	A person who has, who claims to have, or is deemed to have knowledge relevant to an event or matter of interest relevant to an investigation.
Witness credibility	A view of the witness's reliability and believability informed by demeanour, consistency of evidence, a chronology of events, history, motivations, and other relevant factors.
Witness evidence	Statements and documents testified to, under oath or affirmation by a person claiming to have factual knowledge of an event or incident.
Workplace	A home, shop, factory, farm or office where a person is employed to render a service to an employer who pays them a salary or wages and sometimes provides additional benefits.
Workplace Harassment	Refers to acts designed by those in power, or part of an inner circle, to force an employee to leave employment or face an injustice and suffer the consequences.
Work product (legal practice)	The writings, notes, memoranda, reports or recorded conversations between a client and a legal representative; also includes research.
Work product privilege	A doctrine that protects all the above products, as advice that may be presented in litigation, by a party's representative or attorney.

In summary

The goal of this chapter was to unlock key concepts and terms from the 7 Steps of Conducting a Best Practice Workplace Investigation model. The intended outcome of this approach is to ensure that the practitioner is empowered to:

- Define the problem, issue or challenge that triggered the investigation by knowing how to apply the concepts and terms used by professionals.
- Conduct research by referencing the organisational policy and using the relevant investigation guide, policy or protocol with clarity of purpose.
- Successfully create a framework for such an investigation, armed with information.
- Interview the complainant, the affected person, as well as witnesses.
- Determine if any workplace policies have been violated or not.
- Consider whether any national employment legislation, or public, or social policy has been breached during the incident or event.
- Draw conclusions of fact and make recommendations regarding substantiation of allegations.
- Report to the employer, based on all the above factors, thus helping the organisation to manage employment risks.

Appendices

1. Fair procedure. Item 4(1) and (4) of the *Code of Good Practice: Dismissal* in Schedule 8 of the LRA, 66 of 1995

(1) Normally, the employer should conduct an investigation to determine whether there are grounds for dismissal. This does not need to be a formal enquiry. The employer should notify the employee of the allegations using a form and language that the employee can reasonably understand. The employee should be allowed the opportunity to state a case in response to the allegations. The employee should be entitled to a reasonable time to prepare the response and to the assistance of a trade union representative or fellow employee. After the enquiry, the employer should communicate the decision taken, and preferably furnish the employee with written notification of that decision.

(4) In exceptional circumstances, if the employer cannot reasonably be expected to comply with these guidelines, the employer may dispense with pre-dismissal procedures.

2. Explanatory Memorandum on the 7 Steps Investigation Platform

Step 1: The Initial Report and the Decision to Investigate

a Stage One

Review organisational guidelines, prescripts, policies and collective bargaining agreements to determine if there is a *prima facie* case to investigate.

b. Stage Two

Decide on the process to be followed – informal / formal investigation.

c. Stage Three

Inform the leadership and management of the organisation and advise on preliminary analysis of issues.

Step 2: Organisation Planning the Investigation

a. Stage One

   Identify allegations to be investigated using an organisational methodology document and investigation protocols.

b. Stage Two

   Prepare terms of reference using the complaint sheet, or a grievance form, including policy and procedure to conduct the investigation.

c. Stage Three

   Appointment of investigator or team of investigators

d. Stage Four

   Develop an investigation plan that identifies witnesses to be interviewed and plan activities to be undertaken.

e. Stage Five

   Analyse whether or not any administrative action is necessary.

Step 3: Investigator Conducting the Investigation

a. Stage One

Conduct interviews with identified witnesses chronologically - with built-in procedural fairness - for compliance with principles of natural justice.

b. Stage Two

Seek to comply with scope and purpose of investigation by referencing specific documents relevant to the investigation.

c. Stage Three

Follow a pre-determined, but flexible list of activities to get the facts including background information on each one of the witnesses.

d. Stage Four

Conduct industry research to incorporate best practice into the investigatory processes.

e. Stage Five

Start building an investigation file, with all the records of received evidence relating to the interviews conducted with interviewees.

Step 4: Reviewing the Received Evidence

a. Stage One

Determine the credibility of each one of the witnesses, using objective criteria.

b. Stage Two

Make findings of fact, based on evidence presented and received from all the witnesses using an analysis of substantiation; not substantiated or inconclusive evidence.

c. Stage Three

Consult with internal legal advisors or the external counsel of the employer, to ensure privileged information is not disclosed unwittingly and the organisation is not exposed to risks.

Step 5: Presenting Initial Findings and Recommendations

a. Stage One

Prepare an interim report for factual comment by the affected person, complainant, and a specific witness, showing bare facts uncovered, hence the present recommendations.

b. Stage Two

Request that above listed persons comment in writing by a specific date, failing which the report will be regarded as a true reflection of the matter under investigation, as per the findings.

c. Stage Three

By the appointed date, revisit interim report and/or received comments (if any). Compare with the notes in the investigation file; consult with subject matter professionals internally; experts externally; legal counsel; specialists or relevant team members if necessary to ensure the report becomes factual, on a balance of probabilities.

Step 6: Submitting the Final Report

a. Stage One

Prepare a structured report that shows and proves that the investigator complied with the organisational and legal guidelines for conducting a workplace investigation.

b. Stage Two

Develop a separate investigation file containing all the evidence collected and received by the investigator, throughout all the stages of the investigation, including the attachments to the actual, final report.

c. Stage Three

Prepare an executive summary based on all the above information and consult with your attorney to determine who it may be shared with, on a need to know basis, given issues of privileged information.

d. Stage Four

Submit the final report to the identified recipients, as per your investigation plan, and in compliance with the necessary internal investigation guidelines consulted at the start of the process.

Step 7: Managing the Investigation Aftermath

a. Stage One (Individuals)

- Depending on the nature of issues that triggered investigation, the leadership of organisation can suggest a one-on-one meeting to address the root cause of the problem between the protagonist and antagonist, after they are informed of the outcome of the investigation.
- Alternatively, the individuals involved can just be informed that the investigation outcome uncovered facts which showed that the allegations are not substantiated; are substantiated or that the evidence is inconclusive, but management will still be taking confidential action which cannot be disclosed; or no action.
- Should anyone be dissatisfied with the outcome, the parties have options that they can exercise, as listed in the different prescripts that management is citing.

b. Stage Two (Team)

- A facilitated meeting can be held between the team and a professional, and management if the investigated issues affected the entire team, in order to repair fractured relationships.
- Encourage parties to rebuild relationships and move forward in building a decent workplace, free from issues that afflicted them.

c. Stage Three (Division)

In the case of an investigation that identified systemic issues, it will be necessary for the employer to sensitise the members and leaders of a division about what was uncovered. Hence the need for a team building initiative to address the main issues and find workable solutions that can be embraced by all.

d. Stage Four (Organisation)

An investigation that uncovers a lack of leadership skills on the part of a layer of management requires that this issue be raised and addressed through interventions including coaching and mentoring, as part of capacity-building.

3. Public Service Commission (SA) Workplace Investigation Protocol Table of Contents

- Preamble
- Statutory provisions
- Guiding principles
- Complaint mechanisms
- Type of investigations
- Pre-engagement activities
- Appointment of investigating officers
- Investigative process
- Drafting of the report
- Publishing and confidentiality of reports
- Monitoring the implementation of the recommendations of the PSC
- Requests for access to information
- Conclusion

NB: This is a summary of the investigation policy and procedure document that is used by the PSC to conduct all categories and types of investigations related to the mandate of the organisation. It is not a dedicated workplace investigation protocol as such.

Nevertheless, it is useful for a comparative analysis of what is currently happening in the South African arena across sectors.

For more information, please see their official website at www.psc.gov.za

4. 7 Best Practice Investigation Principles

Principle 1: Confidentiality

Maintaining confidentiality is critical to the integrity of an investigation. Failing to ensure strict confidentiality throughout all phases of an investigation can have very serious consequences, e.g.:

a. Someone's reputation may be damaged if others learn of the allegation(s) made regardless of whether the allegations are found to be true or not.
b. The success of an investigation can be undermined if others know of the investigation.
c. The investigation subject might engage in cover-up activities when they learn they are being investigated.
d. The employer might be vulnerable to negative publicity or liability.
e. The employer obligations to and/or relationship with a government agency and/or regulators may be prejudiced if information is communicated at an inappropriate time.
f. The disclosure of information or misinformation may cause retaliatory action.

Although the need for confidentiality begins with receiving an allegation, it does not end with the conclusion of an investigation.

The fact that an investigation is underway or is being considered; the subject matter of it; the process followed; and the materials or information gathered including the results of the investigation must always be treated confidentially.

This includes being very careful before using the details of an investigation at some later point in time (e.g. for training purposes), if these details could identify the individuals / business units / directorates involved. Best practice requires that a competent investigator knows what to share, with whom and when.

At the outset of an investigation, meet with the investigation leader to ensure you understand his communication and investigation plans and have identified those with whom you can discuss the investigation, in whole or in part.

Throughout the investigation actively maintain confidentiality.

Never discuss the facts of an investigation or its contents with anyone other than those identified by the investigation leader as being in the need to know list. If you feel that (either in a personal or professional capacity) you need to discuss the matter with someone not on the 'need to know' list, you should first discuss the matter with your investigation leader.

Resist the curiosity of others – even those more senior than you – as curiosity is not a basis for sharing any information about an investigation.

Maintain the security of documents / evidence (in hard or soft copy) which are relevant to the investigation, including those produced by interviewees, the investigation subject and the employer as well as those generated as part of the investigation. Prevent unauthorised access to them by others.

Mark all documents you create and send with the appropriate and confidentiality notifications, but (as noted in the section on documents), do not mark on or otherwise alter original documents in any way.

It is especially important to conduct interviews in as confidential a manner as possible. Always remember:

a. Be particularly conscious when communicating about an investigation via e-mails; it is too easy for emails to be moved or forwarded to others. Where possible, avoid using actual names or the subject or persons involved in the investigation; mark emails as confidential. Do not forward.

b. Explain to each interviewee that maintaining confidentiality is mandatory including why. At the time of the interview, either give a copy of the "fairness and confidentiality in internal investigations" statement to each interviewee or talk them through the contents. However it is handled, a written record should be created and maintained in the investigation file.

c. Consider whether it might be appropriate to ask individuals not directly involved in the investigation, but who are aware of it, to give an undertaking that they will keep all matters related to the investigation confidential. If in doubt about whether you should ask for this, consult the investigation leader.

d. If asked whether the employer will keep his identity / evidence confidential, explain that you will make every effort to do so, but that disclosure may be necessary for the purposes of the investigation. This may be because the organisation may be legally required to disclose it, or because the employer may wish to do so as part of its commitment to cooperate with a regulator or government agency.

e. Explain that you will provide information about the allegation to legal counsel and appropriate persons in the organisation as part of the investigation process.

Principle 2: Professionalism

The essence of professionalism is that you conduct yourself and your investigation in a professional manner, i.e. with integrity, fairness and diligence. Professionalism spans many of the attributes presented in principles such as competence, confidentiality, timeliness and objectivity.

The investigator's performance in investigating reflects the professionalism of the organisation. Often the integrity of the investigation is judged by the investigation of the investigator(s), e.g., the way that you conduct an interview sets the perception that you and the employer take the investigation seriously, mean what you say and will do what you say will do.

Acting with professionalism means treating everyone involved with respect, knowing how to say no in a firm but polite way and recognising the limits of your contribution to the investigation. It is crucial to know how to ask for help when you need it; it is not a failure to admit that you need guidance or other assistance.

Recognising your limits also means knowing when to accept decisions you do not agree with. Constructive dissent is useful in the planning stages of an investigation, but once a course of action is decided upon – even if it is not your personal preference – you must execute it with a positive attitude. Of course, if you think the decision is improper, you should raise it with the Investigation Leader. Equally, if you think the investigation plan involves illegal, unethical and/or unprofessional conduct or have any questions you should raise it with the Director: HRM.

Principle 3: Competence

The quality of an investigation depends largely on the competency of the investigator. The purpose of each investigation is to determine the facts by conducting an impartial, thorough, professional investigation.

If the allegations are substantiated, appropriate disciplinary action will be decided upon and administered by others; your role is to find the facts and present them in a clear and concise manner so that the decision makers are equipped to take an appropriate decision.

Competence is developed over time, through education and experience. Use the skills required of the Investigation Leader as your competence goal. Subject matter knowledge helps build self-confidence and listening skills; you will not be distracted by trying to understand what the interviewee is talking about and can instead listen to what is being said.

Best practice says that the key to being competent is to know what you are doing. Build your competence throughout your career as an investigator. More importantly:

a. Undergo investigation training.
b. Seek out subject matter training to learn the risk areas and red flags.
c. Understand organisational standards including what they mean in practice.
d. Practice preparing the papers you will present, e.g., draft notes/reports that are clear and concise.
e. Enhance your employer and industry knowledge.
f. Prepare, prepare, prepare. Think in advance about what situations might be presented to you and how you will deal with them. For example, anticipate the questions you are likely to be asked by an interviewee and how you will respond to them.
g. Be inquisitive. An investigation can sometimes take an unexpected course and you should be keen to follow relevant leads you are given.
h. Practice stepping back from a situation so that you can separate the overall scope of the investigation from the detail you are involved in.
i. Think in advance about how your time can be used most efficiently.
j. Be open to learning from colleagues. Other investigators will have a wealth of experience you can learn from.

Principle 4: Prevent Retaliation

It is fundamental that those who are the source of a complaint and/or those who cooperate in an investigation be protected from retaliation. A person will only provide information if they believe they will not be penalised for doing so.

The investigator needs to be alert to signs of retaliation.

Remember that retaliation can happen at any time, not only after an incident is reported or an investigation is started. It can also take many forms. For example:

a. A negative performance evaluation.
b. A failure to be given a promotion opportunity.
c. Receiving lower quality work assignments.
d. Being excluded from meetings and decision making.
e. A reduced level of salary increase, bonus or other pay treatment.
f. Being taunted or ostracised by colleagues or a manager.
g. The person or their property being subjected to harm.

Best practice requires that, as an investigator, you need to be alert to the nuances of retaliation including how to deal with it. This requires that the investigator:

a. Anticipate who may become the target of retaliation in your investigation.
b. Remind the relevant managers of individuals who may be the target of retaliatory behaviour, to be aware of the risk and their obligation to prevent and/or stop retaliation of any kind.
c. Remind each person interviewed that any person who, in good faith, seeks advice, raises a concern, reports misconduct or cooperates in an investigation is following the organisation's Code of Conduct or Employee Handbook and doing the right thing. The employer will not tolerate retaliation against such a person.
d. Make sure an interviewee understands that the organisation's non-retaliation policy is enforced vigorously.
e. Make it clear that individuals engaging in retaliatory conduct will be subject to disciplinary action, which may include dismissal.

f. If an individual alleges he has been the victim of retaliation you must immediately raise it with the investigation leader.

Principle 5: Impartiality

Investigations are conducted to determine facts upon which decision makers can decide an outcome. Both investigators and decision makers aim to better protect the organisation including its employees.

An investigation must be conducted by those who do not have an interest in the matter they are investigating, nor an appearance of a conflict of interest.

Impartiality means that everyone gets a fair chance and that all investigation subjects are investigated in the same manner, with the same professional, impartial and objective treatment.

Principle 6: Objectivity

Throughout our lives, most of us develop a sense of right and wrong; a set of values. These values influence the way we live and the decisions we make. They are our own and therefore they are subjective.

An investigation in contrast must be objective that is free of opinion and bias. All information must be reviewed and analysed using the same standards. Additionally, the findings in an investigation should be based on the facts, not an opinion filtered through the investigator's value system.

The purpose of an investigation is to find the facts so others can assess:

a. Whether there is evidence of a violation of law, company policies and procedures or the Code of Conduct.
b. What the causes of any violations are; and,
c. What opportunities there are to improve the corporate compliance programme. The purpose of an investigation is not to determine what

should occur as a result of the findings. While the investigator may make recommendations about whether or how management should take the matter further, it is not the role of the investigator to make or implement decisions about what sanctions, if any, should be applied following the investigation.

Objectivity helps to guarantee that every employee is treated the same. Best practice makes no assumption about whether the investigation subject, an interviewee or person reporting the matter, is right or not. The job of the investigator does not include taking sides, but to objectively find out what happened.

Do not:

a. Jump to conclusions or have a predetermined view of the case outcome.
b. Consider providing a predetermined victory. Proving an allegation is unfounded is as much a successful resolution as proving someone acted wrongly.

Do:

a. Examine different theories of the case.
b. Get more information rather than drawing conclusions from inadequate information.
c. Remember that your goal is to determine the facts only.

Principle 7: Timeliness

Investigations vary in their level of complexity, including the length of time they take to complete. However, they all have one thing in common, that is the need to be carried out promptly.

Timeliness is part of conducting your investigation professionally, but it is specifically important for other reasons, namely:

a. Wrongly accused people should be cleared as quickly as possible.

b. Corrective action is generally more effective when taken closer to the trigger event.
c. Ongoing wrongdoing must be stopped as quickly as possible.
d. You will assist in defending any investigation / legal action that arises in connection with the investigation or the matter underlying it.

Timeliness of an investigation will be unique to that investigation. Your investigation leader will set a timetable that gives a reasonable amount of time to conduct the investigation. You should work within the timetable. If, for any reason, the investigator cannot keep to the timetable you should notify the investigation leader immediately.

The investigation leader may need to contact individuals awaiting the outcome or give an update of the investigation, or to draw upon other resources to address the matter. Best practice requires that the investigator:

a. Speak up if they think insufficient time has been allocated to carry out interviews / tasks associated with the investigation.
b. You must not compromise the quality of an investigation by completing it quickly or if you feel pressured to give your findings prematurely.
c. The deeper you need to delve to get the facts, the longer the investigation may take.
d. Interviews may also be delayed when people are travelling, are on holiday or on medical leave.
e. Speak to the investigation leader to get the time necessary to complete a thorough investigation.
f. Be prompt in making contact with and/or interviewing the person who made the initial complaint / report (if known). Use good judgement to establish a timeframe for making such contact. This contact should occur within 24 hours if the matter involves a potential threat to the person, property or the environment; within three business days if the matter appears time sensitive but is not an emergency; and within two

weeks for non-time sensitive matters.

g. Act quickly to ensure that relevant documents, evidence and records or communications are retained. Speak up immediately if at any time during the investigation (be it during an interview, a review of documents or evidence) you become aware of an illegal act, ongoing illegal activity or an imminent threat to property or person. In this case you should immediately contact the investigation leader to take any action required to address the non-compliance or threat.
h. Do not agree to a timetable you cannot meet. More importantly, use your time efficiently.

Do not view an investigation as who can close out the greatest number of cases fastest. It is not a contest with colleagues. You are appointed to conduct a thorough investigation in the shortest reasonable amount of time.

5. Typical evidence sources

- Documents
- Witnesses
- Employee handbook
- Applicable laws
- Organisational policies
- Industry good practice relating to investigations of incidents and events
- Analogical instruments
- Anecdotal evidence
- Character evidence
- Circumstantial evidence
- Demonstrative evidence

- Digital evidence

6. Investigation interview framework

- Planning the interview
- Arranging the interview
- Opening the interview
- Conducting the interview
- Asking questions
- Tips for interviewing different parties

7. Model Workplace Investigation Plan

- Investigation overview
- Scope and purpose
- Resources
- Time frame
- Affected person(s)
- Responsibilities
- Risk management
- Information gathering tasks

8. Structure: Final Workplace Investigation Report

COVER PAGE

CASE NO: ______________________________

Date: ______________________________

Location: ______________________________

Business Unit / Function: ______________________________

Introduction: ______________________________

____

____

Allegations: ______________________________

____

____

Issues: ______________________________

____

____

Investigation Approach: ______________________________

____

____

Chronology: ______________________________

____

____

Investigator Analysis: ______________________________

____

____

Non-retaliation steps taken: ______________________________

____

____

Expert opinions (where appropriate) and precedents:

____

____

Documentation: ____

____

Control weaknesses and opportunities to improve compliance programme

____

____

____

CONTENTS

Introduction

Terms of reference

Investigation process (Methodology)

Findings

Issues of concern in the evidence

Analysis / Conclusions

Recommendations

Index of appendices

9. Principles for Conducting Workplace Investigation Interviews

- Advise the employee that the investigator represents the employer.
- Inform affected persons about the general purpose and process of the investigation.
- Emphasise that the investigation is a fact finding exercise only, seeking to find the truth regarding allegations or complaints.

- Remind the interviewee upfront of the importance of telling the truth and full disclosure.
- Reassure all parties that the employer will not tolerate retaliation or intimidation of witnesses.
- Even though the interview is confidential, a report will be made to the employer and law enforcement agencies if a crime is suspected.
- A witness has a contractual responsibility to cooperate with an employer investigation.
- The investigator has a responsibility to preserve documents.
- Affected person(s) has the right to a support person or representation during the investigation, subject to limitations.
- Start with open-ended questions.
- Periodically summarise and review answers.
- Concentrate on the facts, using a chronological path.
- Ask follow-up questions, to clarify contradictions.
- Listen to the witness when he responds to questions.
- Take clearly written and legible notes.
- Consider getting written statements.
- Prepare a summary of the interview.

Bibliography

Anon, 2003. *Best practises in workplace investigations,* New York: American Bar Association.

Anon, 2008. *Local government industry.*

Grogan, J., 2012. *Dismissal.* 3rd Edition ed. Johannesburg : Juta.

Guerin, L., 2016. *Essential guide to workplace investigations - A step by step guide to handling employee complaints and problems.* 4th Edition ed. California, Nolo Publishers.

Malouf, D., 2003. *How to teach adults in a fun and exciting way.* 2nd Edition ed. Autstralia, Allen & Unwin.

Morich, G. B., 2008. *Workplace investigation guide.* I-sight.

Mzangwa, T., 2015. *Legislation and employment relations in South Africa.* Journal of governance and regulation, Unisa.

Woslain Linda B, B. S. M., 2018. *Best Practices in conducting internal workplace investigations of discrimination and harassment complaints.* Employee Relations Law Journal, 44(2).

Endnotes

Chapter 1

1. Annual reports of the CCMA and Public Sector Bargaining Councils (GPSSBC & PSCBC) as well as the Public Service Commission South Africa for the period 2016 – 2018
2. Ogletree, Denkins, 2015. *Top 10 workplace investigation mistakes.* Volume Part 1.
3. Stam, I. I., 2018. *Don't underestimate the investigation process.* South African Labour guide
4. Anon, Just the Facts - Workplace investigations and documentation. s.l.:Veryll Dama LLP.
5. Ogletree, Denkin LLP, *Conducting an effective workplace investigation.*
6. National Labour Relations Board Rulings (2017).
7. Ellis L, B. L., 2014. Documenting and presenting workplace investigations. AWI, 5(4).
8. Ellis L, B. L., 2018. How to conduct an investigation. SHRM.
9. Anon, *Workplace investigation follow up checklist.* I-sight .
10. Anon, *The one thing you should do after investigation.* Work Logic .

Chapter 2

1. Benton & Keller, Workplace law – *Do's and Don'ts of workplace investigations*
2. Article in a journal – Merick, Craig, Bloch, *Guide to conducting workplace investigations* – 2008,
3. Article in a journal – California Association of workplace investigations Inc, Carey Corbaley, - name of journal CAOWI - , 2010, title of article – who should conduct a workplace investigation – an internal or external investigator?
4. Managing Workplace Investigations. A Practical Guide for the Queensland Public Sector, Australian Government. 2018
5. Collective bargaining agreement signed between the recognised unions in the public service, with the State as employer.
6. Public Service Commission (SA) Workplace Investigation Protocol

Chapter 3

1. Grogan, J, 2012, *Dismissal*, 3rd edition. Johannesburg, Juta and Co.
2. Ballard A and Eastel P, (2018), 'Procedural Fairness in Workplace investigations', *Alternative Law Journal*
3. Code of good practice dismissal. Schedule 8 of the *Labour Relations Act* 66 of 1995.
4. PSC (2007 - 2008), *Grievance strengths in the public service*, Pretoria.
5. Bradley, Werksman, Davis (2009),– 'Workplace bullying – Remedies and recourse in South African Law'. *Werksman Attorneys.*
6. Griesel J, 'Sexual harassment in the workplace. Journey – Top Tips for HR journal'
7. 'Sexual harassment as a form of discrimination in employment', *Women's Legal Centre SA*, Cape Town.

8. Baxter R and McCarville R, (2017), 'Key steps for a workplace investigation'.
9. Smit D M, (2019), 'Bullying in the workplace – towards a uniform approach in SA Labour Law', *University of Free State*
10. Guerin L, 2016. *The essential guide to workplace investigations – a step by step guide to handling employee complaints and problems*, 4th edition, USA
11. *Labour Relations Act* nu 66 of 1995

Chapter 4

1. '6 steps for successful incident investigation.' *Risk Tec.*
2. *Cananda Labour Code* – part 2
3. Ballard A and Eastel P, (2018), 'Procedural fairness in workplace investigations'. *Alternative Law Journal*
4. Hudson D, (2019), 'Evidence collection – tips for workplace investigations', *Queens University,* Australia.
5. Muller D, (2009), 'How to conduct fair HR investigations (6 best practices)', *HR Acuity,* I-sight.

Chapter 5

1. Oregon State government. *Investigation toolkit.* 2018
2. Conell Diana and others, 'Conducting effective internal investigations', *Association of Corporate Counsel of America.*
3. 'Tackling poor performance', (2004), *Institute for employment studies*
4. 'Best practised in workplace investigations, (2003), *American Bar Association*
5. 'Local Government industry guidelines on workplace investigations', Australia

6. '6 points investigation process', *I-sight*
7. Duffy JP, (2008), 'Fundamentals of conducting workplace investigations'
8. Murphy AP and Van den berg QH, (2002), 'How to conduct a fraud investigation' *HR Advisor*
9. 'Conducting internal investigations', *BC Human Rights organisation*
10. Coxwell PC, (Nov 2002) 'A multi dismary approach to corporate fraud and investigations' *LPM Magazine*
11. Cressey D, (1973), 'Other people's money' *Montclair Patterson Smith*
12. Lomer D, (2018), 'How to conduct a workplace investigation – step by step', *I-sight*

Chapter 6

1. Stam, I I, 'Don't underestimate the investigations process', S*A Labour guide*
2. Scopelliti V, (Feb 2019), 'How fact finding and disiplinary investigation differ, *Wise workplace journal*
3. 'Planning a workplace investigation', *Work logic*
4. Sacks, Tierney, (Sept 2012), 'Confidentiality in investigations – a trap for unweary employers', *Sacks, Tierney Attorneys*
5. 'Investigation interviews – a best practises guide', *I-sight*
6. 'Documenting and preserving workplace investigations', Oct 2014), *AWI Journal*, (Volume 5 – issue nu 4)
7. Lomer D, (2017), '44 investigation interview questions for the complainant, the subject and witnesses', *I-sight.*
8. Lomer D, (2017), '44 investigation interview questions for the complainant, the subject and witnesses', *I-sight.*
9. Lomer D, (2017), '44 investigation interview questions for the complainant, the subject and witnesses', *I-sight.*

10. Lomer D, (2017), '44 investigation interview questions for the complainant, the subject and witnesses', *I-sight.*
11. Lomer D, (2017), '44 investigation interview questions for the complainant, the subject and witnesses', *I-sight.*
12. Lomer D, (2017), '44 investigation interview questions for the complainant, the subject and witnesses', *I-sight.*

Chapter 7

1. 'Collecting evidence', *Wise workplace*
2. Actual case study where the names of the parties was changed.
3. Item 4 subparagraph 1 of the *Code Of Good Practice Dismissal* in schedule 8 of the Labour Relations Act 66 of 1995
4. 'The first information is almost always wrong', Consultants – *Cosmos*
5. 'Documenting and preserving workplace investigations', (Oct 2014), *AWI Journal*, Volume 5 issue 4
6. Baxter R and McCarville R, '5 key steps for a proper workplace investigation'.
7. Lomer D, 'The ultimate guide to writing investigation reports', *I-sight*

Chapter 8

1. Naidoo S, (2016), 'South African criminal law response to the crime to fraud and corruption in local government', *University of Pretoria*
2. Vos, Solomon and Kruk, 'Corporate Crime Fraud and Investigation in South Africa'
3. Naicker K, (2006) 'White collar crime in South Africa', *University of Johannesburg*

4. Lonmin Mines Policy on Fraud and Investigation
5. Minnaar J, (2006), 'Understanding fraud and white collar crime', *University of Johannesburg*
6. Donald Cressey, 'Other peoples money'

Chapter 9

1. Jones G, (2016), 'Report writing for HR Professionals conducting workplace investigations'. *CPHR* Alberta.
2. Scopelliti V, (aug 2017) 'What evidence should be in a workplace investigation report', *Wise Workplace*
3. Oregon state government investigations toolkit – 2018
4. 'Prevention of harassment in the workplace', *HR policy manual,* Canadian Red Cross Society
5. Janove JW, (Aug 2004), 'Legal trans – conclude and communicate', *SHRM magazine*
6. Henry T, 'Resend investigation cases – the employers duty of care towards its employees during a workplace investigation', *Work Logic.*

Chapter 10

1. 2017, 'Employment practice solutions and workplace insiders', *Synercy workplace investigations*
2. Bryant-Smith R, '10 best practice interventions post investigation', *Work Logic*
3. Donalds B, (Aug 2017), 'Shifting from workplace investigations to restoration', *ADR institute*, (Ontario, Canada)
4. Carrier S, (2017), 'Effective ways to improve workplace culture and dynamics following a workplace investigation', *Work Logic*

5. Pizzo R, (Dec 2018), 'Putting Humpty Dumpty back together again – restoring teams after workplace investigations' *Queens University.*
6. Pizzo R, (Dec 2018), 'Putting Humpty Dumpty back together again – restoring teams after workplace investigations' *Queens University.*

Chapter 11

1. Malouf, D., 2003. *How to teach adults in a fun and exciting way.* 2nd Edition ed. Autstralia, Allen & Unwin
2. Miller, Richard, Dr. (2006), 'Building a Successful Community of Practice', *Miller-Klein Associates Ltd*
3. In the Author's Preface it is written that there are no accredited workplace investigation training programmes in South Africa. The related courses referred to therein are developed and run by: NOSA; Oxbridge; National School of Government; University of Pretoria and the SAPS. All of them are generic or subject specific programmes that have a small reference to conducting a workplace investigation. We can refererence training courses done by Accociation of Certified Fraud Examiners (ACFE).
4. In contrast to the position at note 3 above, the following international organisations all run professional workplace investigation courses: SHRM (USA); EEOC(USA); ERC (Australia); WISE Workplace (Australia); HRPA (USA) and i-HR Australia among others.
5. All the above organisations run programmes relating to Advanced Investigation Techniques; Specialisation courses in Investigating Sexual Harassment; Workplace Abuse of Executive Power as well as Workplace Bullying and Victimisation Investigations
6. See, Billet: "Learning in the Workplace" 2001 for an illustration of the Tell/Show/Do/Review model of learning and teaching and G.Robothan "Learning how to facilitate learning". Undated article

7. See, Appendix 2 where the 7 Steps for Conducting Workplace Investigations are explained
8. This is an illustration of a typical Basic Workplace Investigation Training Programme
9. This is another illustration of an advanced Workplace Investigations Course
10. This is the outcome of a programme where participants (professionals) share their experiences from the field with a facilitator who has technical competencies, in order to enrich the workplace investigation theory and practice. For additional information, see: "Cambridge Advanced Learner's Dictionary and Thesaurus."
11. SHRM Magazine article written by Dori Meinert, "How to Conduct a Workplace Investigation", April 21/2017
12. WISE Workplace Training Programme titled, "Conducting Workplace Investigations" (Advanced)

About the Author

Tommy Thamsanqa Bangani is a multidisciplinary professional and entrepreneur who started his professional career as a trade union official at the South African Commercial, Catering and Allied Workers Union (SACCAWU) in Cape Town in 1990. During his seven year stint at SACCAWU he filled various positions, including Western Cape regional secretary, educator and collective bargaining coordinator. He joined the Department of Labour as a public sector manager where he respectively started and led two business units, namely the reconstituted Inspections and Enforcement Services (IES) and later the Labour Market Information, Statistics and Planning Unit (LMIS).

Not one to shy away from a new challenge, Bangani transitioned into the private sector where he worked for Deloitte and Touché, Human Capital Corporation as an Employee Relations Consultant and later moved into the financial services sector as a Corporate Affairs Manager and subsequently as a Business Development Manager for Old Mutual (SA).

He held the position of Director for Employee Relations within the Police, Roads and Transport Department with the Free State Provincial Government before taking on his latest challenge. He is currently a partner in a professional services consulting and training firm, Somila Sisonke, as well as a founding member of a legal protection insurance business known as Sisonke Group Legal Services.

Made in the USA
Monee, IL
05 November 2026

68020982R00173